Scream Blue Living
NEW AND SELECTED POEMS

OTHER BOOKS BY ROBERT PRIEST

The Mad Hand
The Man Who Broke Out of the Letter X
Sadness of Spacemen
The Visible Man

FOR CHILDREN

The Ruby Hat
The Short Hockey Career of Amazing Jany

Scream Blue Living
New and Selected Poems

by Robert Priest

The Mercury Press

ACKNOWLEDGEMENTS

The author thanks the Toronto Arts Council, the Ontario Arts Council, the
Canada Council for the Arts, and the Department of Communications for their
financial support during the writing of many of these poems.
Thanks to my friends, fans, and family for their love, support,
and inspiration throughout my life.

Poems collected here for the first time previously appeared in: *ARC* ("Flag");
Cross-Canada Writers' Quarterly ("A Cultural Nightmare"); *Poets Against the War*
("Modified Famous Phrases"); and *NOW Magazine* ("The Tree").

The publisher gratefully acknowledges the financial assistance of the Canada
Council and the Ontario Arts Council as well as that of the Ontario Ministry
of Culture and Communications through the Ontario Publishing Centre.

Cover design: Gordon Robertson
Cover photograph: Paul Till
Editor for the press: Beverley Daurio

Typeset in Berkeley Book and Gill Sans by TASK.
Printed and bound in Canada.

Canadian Cataloguing in Publication:

Priest, Robert, 1951-
Scream blue living : new and selected poems
ISBN 0-920544-92-4
I. Title.
PS8581.R47S28 1992   C811'.54   C92-094535-X
PR9199.3.P753S28 1992

The Mercury Press
137 Birmingham Street
Stratford, Ontario
Canada N5A 2T1

Dedicated to Marsha Kirzner
and with thanks to my mother
who recited "The Highwayman"

Contents

Revolutions 11
Friend 12
Poem for Ursula in
   New York 13
Poem 14
Translations 15
Meditation on a Ruler 16
Cigarettes 17
The Door Knob 18
The Hammer 18
Flags 19
What Dew Is 20
Little Heart of My Heart 21
The Change 22
You Want Her 23
If 24
Signatures 25
A Tall Man Walking Fast 25
What Ugly Is 26
On Genuflection 27
Mommies 28
Are There Children 30
An Unidentified Man 31
Target Practice 32
Lesser Shadows 33
The Re-assembled Atom 35
Excuses 36
Concerning My Obsession
   with Blood 37
A Poem about Water 38
Ode to the Clitoris 39
Ode to the Penis 40
Ode to the Bum 41
To His 20th Century Lover 41
Poem for a Dark Woman 42

When My Faith Leaps 43
Birth 44
Slight Exaggeration of a
   Childhood Incident 45
Adolescence 46
My Grandfather Lives 48
My Infected Rainbow 49
Candles 50
The Man behind the Bees 51
The Retroactive Orphan 53
The Ancestry 54
Thirst 55
The Childhood Pin 56
His Little Mother 57
My Therapeutic Cock 58
On the Assembly Line 59
Astrology and
   the Blood Shadow 60
All the Sounds a Scared
   Man Hears 61
Why You Have the Maps 62
Sadness of Spacemen 63
The Television 64
Sultan of the Snowflakes 65
Points 66
The Cup of Words 67
The Kiss I Just Missed 68
Since You Left 69
Hold Me 70
Come to Me 72
Crumbs 73
Ode to Your Mouth 74
Falling through the Heart 75
Proposal 76
More! 77

Contents (Continued)

Disguises 78
Insomnia 79
The Longer Bed 80
Cherries 81
Peaches 82
Mangoes 83
Dec. 8, 1980 84
Ghost Removal 86
How to Pray to a Woman 87
How to Pray to a Toilet 88
Sweet and Sour Angel Wings 89
Christ Is the Kind of Guy 90
Getting Close to God 92
The Starved Man 93
Questions about the Wine 94
Oppress the Oppressed 95
Testament of a New Faith 96
Go, Gather Up the Love 97
Blue Pyramids 98
In the Next War 99
Beautiful Money 100
Report on the Earth-Air
    Addicts 101
The Arms Race of Obbagga 102
The Grizzums 103
Paper 104
Paper II 105
Secrets of Paper 106
Ink 107
Literary Party 108
The Escaped Cock 109
Precautionary Chandeliers 110
The Uncatchable Man 111
Moth 113
My Body 114

Poem for a Fisherwoman
    1983 115
Tales of a Domestic Heart 116
Poem for a Tall Woman 118
Now There Is Rain 119
The Man with the
    Nitroglycerine Tears 120
Sometimes There Is a Way 121
Eggshell Children 122
The School behind
    the School 123
Poète 124
Adventures of My Hand 125
The Man Who Broke Out
    of the Letter X 126
The Birth of a Tree 127
The Mad Hand 128
My Huge Voice 130
Fear of Hands I 131
Fear of Hands II 133
My Father's Hands 134
In Stupid School 135
I Knew I Could Sing (Industrial
    Accident No. 1) 136
Why I Crushed My Hand 137
Industrial Accident No. 2 139
Little Hurts 140
The Violent Man's Hand 141
Poetry Is... 142
Colours of Bullshit 143
Several Other Uses
    for a Halo 144
In Drug Heaven 146
To Me, Eating a Piece
    of Meat 147

Contents (Continued)

My Problem with the Flag 148
My Problem with the Canadian
    National Anthem 149
Silence Is Coming 150
Consumption 151
My Infected Television 153
The Little Pig of Self
    Respect 154
An Exhortation to Dance 155
sperm sperm sperm 157
The Origin of "Woman" 158
Poem for My Unborn Child 159
On the Birth of My Son 160
New Father 160
Your Cry 161
Giant of the Cookycrumbs 163
On hearing that Gandhi tested
    his Brahmacharya by sleeping
    with young girls 164
Love as though 165
Sleep Poem 166

Difficult Heaven 168
poem cross canada 169
The Opening 170
Babyness before Words 171
My Mother's Hands 172
Zend Elegy   174
In Memoriam: Ellen Priest 175
Everybody Gets Up... 177
The House behind
    the Theatre 178
Autumn of Hands 179
Flag 180
A Cultural Nightmare 181
The Tree 182
The Environmental
    Leap Forward 183
Modified Famous Phrases 184
Fictinos: Time Release
    Poems 185
Homebirth 189
INDEX 191

Revolutions

(for Galileo)

i am a tall white thing that birds fly out of
that is why you see me in the morning so open-mouthed and foolish
the doctor said
"you are upside down
you have a large wounded thing in your mouth
i would advise you to cry"
but i said "no doctor
you are wrong
i am tremulous and exultant— a green strand
drawn from the throat of a flower
i am the magnet the wind arrives at finally
those are songs you see lodged in me
if i cry there will be no passion in it
i have tried again and again to throw off these robes of water
but wherever i have whirled them—
there the drunken— the inexhaustible flowers
have followed and come groping up to me
with praises
why should i cry?"
"you're upside down" he said
"no" i replied, and i began to revolve in the air
in front of him
"you think it must be somewhere near here
that the ground is
the suicides have told you
the rain and snow have told you
it's down below
somewhere under the houses
but they are wrong
and you are wrong
i am that dancing man
who kicks over the jug of the stars
those are my tracks across the moon

wherever i put my feet
that is where
the ground is

Friend

(for George Kerr)

somewhere between old yeller
and pythias you stand
firm in my closest friendship

the honesty comes from you in words
while i push mine out
with a typewriter
hardly daring to touch the keys

i see something of the earth in you
the hardy peasant
who does not dream of beanstalks
as he tills the drying soil
the calloused hand
which will not chafe
on fantasies

i am such a flightier crow than you
i ask to grow the dove's wings
as you shake your head
and look for another worm

our friendship is
that we know what friendship is
that we have looked for gods
but not in each other
that we have battered the idols
but not one another

Poem for Ursula in New York

i will imagine that your mouth
now tastes of apples, Ursula
just by chance, in that you have just
bitten into one.
i will imagine that you have left
your room immediately
determined to overcome your fear of
the streets
you are right in the centre of the city
and all the traffic of the world
is moving round you
i imagine you feel a little like
swirling your skirts
strolling in your outrageous way
down some street
and the wild energy climbs your body
like a crackling ecstatic light, lifts your
breasts, it flings your hair, stares
amazed into your eyes and coming finally
on your man, whatever man, (may he be
gentle with you) leave him like a white moth
just brushed by a hint of colour
with that taste,
that aroma of apples
lingering on his lips

Poem

like two branches
locked in skins of ice
my arms are made beautiful
with reaching for her
i want something impossible
entangled in them
and it becomes me

o she has breasts, world
small breasts
that tilt up
into something in me
that overflows

every day
by her laughter in the house
by her eyes seeing me
by her gentle hands upon my body
i am made more beautiful

and when she lies naked on my bed
there's not a field of wheat
or slender stem of anything
can rival
the slender golden way
i am
as i bend
to kiss her

Translations

i have come to understand
the language of a hand
held limp in mine
while others speak with fingers moving
in a palm

i know the subtle speech of women
that is spoken without sound
or touch, across a room
with only eyes meeting

Even the cryptic rhythms
of my body's secret speaking
with the brain,
the music of memory,
the fearful rhetoric of muscle
moving in a jaw,
or laughter coded
in a severed throat
i understand

but there are tongues—
the simple feeling speech of beasts,
the syllabub of leaf and stem
or seasons turning
through my young age
with which i find no common root,
no dialect or metre—
A speech that has its meaning
only in the moment of its saying
and is then lost forever
senseless as the random marks of birds upon a beach

and so
in still moments, alone
i strain to hear the sounds
of grass growing
or a seed bursting through
the round voices of a shattered stone

and i make my small marks upon the page

Meditation on a Ruler

a ruler is very democratic
for it is divided equally
among its twelve inches
no one inch having more than another

and, as it is, this, a tool
can be used constructively
or destructively
as when a master
slaps some erring schoolboy's hand

a ruler has an edge and a blade.
it is like a man in that it is divided
but unlike a man in that each fragment
is not pitted against the other
nor does it inflict
with a plague of divisions
the world about it
but rather can be used
to join two sundered points
with a straight unerring line

finally,
a ruler,
when you hold it up against the sun
is unlike our cities and our politics,
our bodies and the clothes of the poor
in that it is definitely made to measure

thank you

Cigarettes

Do king-sized cigarettes
yield king-size happiness
Grow queen-sized breasts
on pubescent chests
and King Kong cocks
on a hairless crotch
or just tomb-sized tumours
and smelly breath?

If cigarettes of royal length
are passed as staffs to peasants
what for love's sake
do emperors inhale—
bus exhausts?
crematorium chimneys?

King-sized smoke
for the lungs of the jester
buggered for a joke
by the king's big sceptre
beware all those
who seek what they lack
in the paper-wrapped poison
of the king-sized pack

in marlboro country
the cowboys lie dead
in their ashtrays

The Door Knob

the door knob teaches centuries
of hands
the art of revolution
we thought of it twisting
off the heads of kings
and when the flowers came out uncurling
as though from circles underground
we thought of it again

the holy door knob
teaches us the art of entry—
rotate the wrist
and great worlds will come
spinning out of it
turn that small knob of brass
and the whole mountain will unravel
like the twisting of a thousand
snakes

The Hammer

the blind hammer
beats its eye
upon the nail.

sight won't break
open in it

can't even see
inside itself

but is just darkness
and a voice that holds
the houses up

Flags

I.
all those stars, those stars
do you think they like that small crammed corner?
that stuffed rectangular galaxy
each one waiting to nova?
o those stars, those stars
do you think they are learning brotherhood there?
efficiently arranged
and fenced in
by the stripes, the stripes, the stripes.

II.
the flags have all been unravelled by the wind
and rewoven
now we have the stitched—
the united frankenstein flag—
the patchwork skin of countries and countries
or the blended— the flag deleted
X'd out by its own profusion
moon flag— memorial to wind
trapped undulation of imaginary airs.

the face flag rippling
in a cheek
o the flags and flags of blood
flapping half-masted
for freedom
o still flag
inscrutable rag
of the sky

What Dew Is

the sea is an urge
she has
on nights too still
when days lie flat out
on her
like sheets of sweet and silent water

the sea is an urge
and mountains are her deep desires
cast out
rain is something
held beyond her
something that she arches up her body
like a bridge to meet
but does not meet

and in the morning
when the buds and roots
are moving in her
when her body trembles like a blade of grass
and dawn breaks
no thread of wanting in her

dew
is her cool way
of being
satisfied

Little Heart of My Heart

little heart of my heart
little heart of the voice stopped
little heart of the hands held back
heart of salt
heart of the small tear in your tear
the small voice in your voice.
O small removable heart
heart scraped off in secrecy
heart of the thin shriek—
the small silver shriek at the bottom of the soul
O small backwards heart
little heart of the kiss stopped

The Change

i keep sending off life
but my messengers are not arriving

the suicides
keep calling out for something
some blood-letting maybe
just let the soul out a little
at the wrists
at the wrists
twist the voice
from its dry rag
just one last time
in pain

o my fools
my children
are babbling in the darkness
crying out
with small sawn voices
for something
they can't have
just let the light in
let the light in a little
at the wrists
at the wrists

and so now i'm changing
my symbols are moving
against my death—
the bird emerges from its shell
half-formed
still raw and shocked
the mouth beats a desperate
wing of blood
against the heart
and whatever it is a horse
means to me
has begun to gallop

You Want Her

you want to be soluble in her
you want to be digested
as you digest her
you want her touch to cool
like melting snow your skin on fire
you want to whirl into the centre of her
star-hearted and impure
you want to be returned
through the dark dot that kindled you
you want to be un-made in her
re-made, and crammed in every corner of her
you want to be a blade of grass in her heart
a blossom rising through her blood
you want to siphon off the chromosome
and alter it in her
you want to be a single speck of blood
a tremor in the compass blade
you want to leap like flame
from places where she touches you
you want her in all her shapes
and moods and sizes
you want her
then and now
you want
her
you want her

If

if i could maim that part in me
which generates this need for you
believe me i would do it

if distances could cut the threads
which tie me to you
how quickly i would put a world
between us

if i could nullify your name
and wrench each memory and vision
of you from its painful place in mind
like some ecstatic madman
in the green grass
i would tear you loose

if by denying gods
i might deny this pain
your name engenders in me
trees would be uprooted in my fury
rivers halted, frozen at the source,
the winds contained, contaminated
with your name

i hack these words from silences
my loudest songs cannot dispel
if i could strike the summer
from its place among the seasons
though i wreck the whirling of the world
to rid myself of memory
my love,
i would

Signatures

already i have forgotten
you
your name blends with other names—
is just a jarring discord
single syllable or many
i forget

this wound i barely feel
its ragged edges
cut with many claws
is your mark there?
i cannot know for sure
the signatures disfigure
one another—
are just a series now
of random gashes
it might have been
one demented cat
one viper
one of anything
with teeth and claws
or many
i forget

A Tall Man Walking Fast

a tall man
   walking fast
   down Queen Street
called out—

                    "HEY UGLY!"

and everybody
   turned around

What Ugly Is

i put on a man mask
and went among the people of earth
in search of what
ugly
means

many years the word had troubled
me, as i listened
over and over
to some of the approximately
four billion
mouth sounds
which these
animals
make

beauty i had come to understand
in stars
in eyes
the silver lapping of the oceans there
but ugly
what did it mean?

unrecognized
never speaking
but always listening
i walked their streets
and cities
i went into their starvations
their working places
deep in mines
i climbed a mountain
and looked into the writings
and holy codes
of their artists

but it wasn't until
i shared quarters with an actual family
and watched in shock
the upbringing of their young
that i realized
ugly
is what happens to something
you don't love
enough

On Genuflection

and in buildings huge enough
to house dinosaurs
they worship a creature so small
that they have to get down on their knees
    to talk to him

Mommies

the prime minister has admitted
he needs his mommy
he is down on the floor of the house of commons
crying like a child
in agreement for once, the leader of the opposition
has likewise admitted
that he needs his mommy
and the two of them are hoping
with the mingling of their griefs
to heal the world

so now the streets are filled with people
who claim to need their mommies—
the flower lady needs her mommy
the fish man needs his mommy
the bus conductor needs his mommy
it seems like everyone
whether he had one
or not
needs his mommy

dejected,
great breasts sagging
dry to their navels
all the mommies
are trying to hide
they are worn out with births
their faces made featureless
with so many rough kisses
their limbs are flat
their hands are empty
and their souls are tired

but it is too late for them
laws are being passed
the prime minister is unhappy
the leader of the opposition is unhappy
the flower lady, and the fish man
and the bus conductor are unhappy
"Let their daughters serve time for them
in factories and bars," they cry

meanwhile, rounding up suspects
the mounties go from door to door
with earnest looks and a mirror
saying
"Do you recognize this woman?"

Are There Children

are there children somewhere
waiting for wounds
eager for the hiss of napalm
in their flesh—
the mutilating thump of shrapnel
do they long for amputation
and disfigurement
incinerate themselves in ovens
eagerly
are there some who try to sense
the focal points of bullets
or who sprawl on bomb grids
hopefully
do they still line up in queues
for noble deaths

i must ask:
are soul and flesh uneasy fusions
   longing for the cut—
   the bloody leap to ether
are all our words a shibboleth for silence—
a static crackle
to ignite the blood
and detonate the self-corroding
   heart
does each man in his own way
plot a pogrom for the species
or are we all, always misled
to war

An Unidentified Man

today
i have a gun
and i want to kill
the man

i have killed the wrong man
a hundred times
i have killed him full of fear
from a hundred windows
a hundred dark doorways
i aim always for the groin
or the heart
i want to make just one man cry
as i have cried
just one voice jump from a broken throat
like my voice jumps

so i have killed the man
i have shot him in the face
and heard him cry from something
that is no longer a mouth
i have blasted heads
like soft rotten fruit
i have broken thighs, wrists,
arms with my bullets.
quick deaths, slow deaths
i want to see just one man die slow
as i have died
and i have killed the wrong man a hundred times

but today is different
my aim is improved
i can see full circle now,
almost into death itself

today i have a gun

Target Practice

(the bull's eye)

the bull's eye is the scapegoat
minus its face
stripped of its uniform and nationality
no religion or name
it is the narrow telescopic end
of the mirror
an accidental twin you can't help
killing again and again,
immortal, eternal there in its circles,
a bland enemy
you can never destroy

the bull's eye is the angel
you go hunting for
when winter comes yet again
it is a flock of fathers
finally made small
a round outlaw in hiding
zeroed in on
and paralyzed

it is the last animal
the last god
the last great love

the bull's eye
is your anger compressed
made efficient and holy
ringed by a dozen haloes
it is the bright erupting dot
of a hatred
that practice only makes
more perfect

Lesser Shadows

the buildings wait for the assassins

the shadows are prepared for them—
they flow like dark sheets
of blood from underneath the doors

there are many vacant rooms
many rifles waiting

soon the assassins begin to arrive
they are all a little crazy
moved by politics or dark desires
they are tense and frightened
but eager, jostling one another
for places at the windows

there are assassins behind bushes
assassins on roofs
and distant hilltops
there are so many assassins
there are assassins crouched
in shadows of assassins

it is good that the victim is young
and wealthy. it is good that
he seems to symbolize something

now they prepare their weaponry
his car goes by
the triggers click
a thousand bullets meet
inside a single head
the skull explodes
the president is dead

silently, some with spittle running
from the corners of their mouths,
some dazed, as though awaking from a trance
the assassins file out of the buildings
past the shocked, staring faces to the highways
past the farthest edges of the sun's descending red
and, as night absorbs the lesser shadows
America absorbs her murderers
completely

The Re-assembled Atom

it was time
there was too much light in the world
there were not enough cities
they had to
they re-assembled the atom

its centre they found
spiralled in a woman's womb
boring like a worm for the ovaries
its planets, each one lodged
at the base of the spine
spun out at the necks
of presidents and kings
bullets found them all
divine bullets
in holy surgery
whales swam ashore in suicidal shoals
to deliver its energy
its leaves were fossil leaves
an old woman disgorged them in a purge
they had its tongue and its moon and its memory
but still half of it was lost
half of it was the man
and half the child
its blood lived in wells
deep beneath the earth
it was half money
half starved
it was time
they stitched it all together
they had to
they called it the frankenstein atom
and waited

Excuses

(for Allende)

There were too many amputated limbs
dancing in the streets
and i had to aid a man divided
by his own hands
Suddenly the air was thick with flies
i would have heard the gunfire
but there was a parade of patriotic gates
and doorways in my street
and just then the shadow of a sparrow fell
It fell for hours
blotting out everything
if you had cried louder
there would have been thunder i'm sure
a dispute about mining rights

i would have heard the gunfire
i might have seen him fall
but i was on the wrong side
of too many borderlines
i would have heard the earth cracking
i would have heard the first
of the excuses

Concerning My Obsession with Blood

if i bite into an apple
and the apple breaks in blood
if i wake up and it is raining blood
if lunatics dance joyously
open-mouthed in blood
if all the palaces and stock exchanges
temple walls and factories shall
reek of blood
if blood shall rot in gutters,
flood the streets
and stain the mountain peaks
and valleys
in its unceasing red monsoon
if blood shall seep up through the soil
and mat the grass
if flags are stiff and clotted
to the staff with blood
if khans and kings,
their emperors and generals
and savage soldiers
shall be glutted, stuffed
and sick with blood

then i will write a poem
about water

A Poem about Water

water is something
i want to make perfectly clear
i want to come clean about water
i'm saying the water is dirty
the holy water
in our hearts and mouths and bellies
water is a gem
we come shivering out of
it is the earth
toiling at the earth
a silver mistress
who lulls with singing
the giant reach of land
to stony slumber
water is the earth
reflecting on itself
a liquid contemplation
of the moon and sun
of the distant stars and abysses
that people looking down
might see the beginning
and the end
of thirst

Ode to the Clitoris

little bud
of nerves
all other limbs
are slaves
to your standing up—
vassals to uplift you
in a holy arch of ivory
you are a point in radar
pulsing out
your sonic bleep
to all extremities
where else in nature
shall i find your like
if not strung out
green and undulating
from some river-splitting
rock
you are the water dropped
a thousand miles
into a wide disjointed
ocean,
dawn's first red tongue
of light
lapping at the wide-spread night
you are the hub
of the body—
the tender, topmost
leaf
of the ecstatic tree
you are a box
of sweet lightning
someone breaks open
with a kiss

Ode to the Penis

O penis
you quintessence of flesh
you are all that skin strives to be
master-servant of the body's yearning
you pop me in and out of ecstasy
like a strobe
o sweet foam in the veins
pump the earth's
rivers round
and cleanse the last dregs
of star-stuff
from my toes and eyes

you god-thing!
body-maker!
brainless voyageur!
the white compacted light is
erupting!
O diver in the unfathomable pink
my heart throbs in your white
sex-light like a crazy bird
my soul lifts up its ancient auric wings
and all my body is a swarm of singing insects
round you

Ode to the Bum

due to my profound
knowledge
of the human soul
i can no longer see
even the most shapely
of bums
as anything
but a manifestation
of
duplicity

To His 20th Century Lover

ah when all the night-times meet
and the firefly novas burst
i'll love you dear til Apocalypse
or for a week (whichever comes first)

Poem for a Dark Woman

i am a metal moth
too bright to look at
diving and diving

if i come away from you
it will be as though from berries
all my edges black
from you
my lips and eyes dark
from you
and it will be a dark
like the moon glows in
like the fields i have walked in
singing

i move with your pulse
always in rhythm
with you
i am tied to your dark
centre part
moored to your thighs
like a bobbing boat

i daub you on my lips like ritual
i bathe my hands in you
and burn
only where you
don't touch me

When My Faith Leaps

when my faith leaps
like a man who has a bird
and lets it go
i leap after it

it keeps bringing me
twigs and things
to build temples on

at first i trusted it
but since the house of Christ
fell down on me
and the house of the cry ate at me
and since lately it's been
bringing me things like
arms, like a heart
and a ghost
and since it just brought me
a face
strangely familiar

when my faith leaps
like a man with a short memory
and an exceedingly long tale
i leap after it

Birth

nothing is ordained
  the infant stifling in the cot
  does not predict
  veins rising
  through an ancient hand
the child upon the pendulum
  hooting for joy
  predicts nothing

the past at least is certain

i am face to face
  with my origin
  my mother's grim face
her sweat upon the pillow
the long-forgotten house of blood
forever closed to me

on this cold hearth
writing in the oracle of the scar
i speak my first shrill prophecy

Slight Exaggeration of a Childhood Incident

when i was two
a garbage man gave me a trumpet

it was a small silver
winding dirty trumpet

and shrieking at my own thunder
like any other prodigy mad with energy

i bellowed down Thames Street
levelling buildings, knocking down churches

with my blasts, of course the neighbours
complained, prodigy or no prodigy

they were having no such slumbers
as their very precious own

disturbed by little manic urchins
such as i was

but my mother in her arrogant way
defied them and sat severely on the porch

watching with pride my short pants parade
go boastfully by

it was the police finally
who had to silence me

arriving on bicycles with bells
and blowing whistles

i was standing on a post
in a circle of my peers

and when the bobby said,
"eaaah ooze makin' oowl 'at noise 'en?"

the circle opened magically before me
and they all pointed and said

"it's him—
it's little Robert Priest."

Adolescence

bitter adolescence
  of the apple
and the blossom in me
  cruel laughter
in the house of the heart
no one knowing anyone
  just gathering with masks
  for the meals and then leaving
  for their lives

and the son asking:
  who is this man standing in my blood
  who has my bloody fingerprints
  upon his throat
  who has taken my full stature
  my straight shoulders
  and deep voice
  whose teeth grit on the gristle
  of my heart
  and drink the black bruise dry
  who is this man who cuts the quick of thought
  and tacks the tongue's root
  to trembling infirmity

  who is this woman whose kisses
  smudge my innocence
  who takes my innocence
  and leaves me in my severed prime
  without a root
  who is this haggard woman
  tangled in my veins, my hair, my voice
  who beckons shadows to my sickness
  who has taken my clear flesh
  and undivided soul
  who is this angry woman
  whose love shames me

and the son grits his teeth against
the family
and the family against the son

bitter adolescence
　of the skylark
and the eagle in his eerie
　awkward adolescence
of the man, so arrogant and angry
　slamming all the doors
in the house of the heart
　leaving for good one day
with a curse and a laugh

My Grandfather Lives

my grandfather lives
in the bluest skies ever
too late for my goodbye kiss
gone now that i have never embraced him
gone—
but young again in memory
returned
to his blessed carpentry

goodbye grandfather
my arms never once went round you
and it is too late now

you have left us
only each other
to embrace

My Infected Rainbow

i took my infected rainbow to the rainbow-doctor
totally white sam
and he said what's wrong with it
so i said well just feel it, it's all misty
and it can't even arch over anything
it just dwindles smaller and smaller each day
leaving little stains in the sky
i can't erase
Perhaps it needs a transfusion he said
have you bled into it lately
no i said it's just not sharp enough
any more so he took some of my yellow blood
and he injected it into the top of the rainbow
and some of my black for the bottom
and slowly i watched the seep of the colour through it
the reinvigorated, the refreshed rainbow
flowing in sediments to its
true brilliance
then when it shone like neon
the doctor darkened his office
and we with our faces lit up
knelt down upon our knees
and so made something
for it to arch over

there he whispered to me
now all you need is a wind surgeon
and a healer of leaves...

O no! i shouted, look—
the colour's running out again
look at the apples!
look at the butterflies!

so he examined the rainbow's wrists
and said
you don't need me
you need rasputin
this rainbow's
a haemophiliac!

Candles

You too have pulled a swindle and thereby gained those illicit eyes—
that criminal vision into yourself. You, with your eye at the keyhole,
you will see every jewel in the body: the heart, the many senses (more
than thought), the mountainous fevers rising up from roots in your
feet, the fear flung from you like a robe and then, every night, by
mistake rolled in again (just the dog of you rolling there), the vision
seen then and again— later in the dream— the double-eye, the eye
cluster inside, many times refracted and examined down to the last
splay of light in the centre— the sphere of colour— and you too
have a brush, or feet to dance, or even a pattern of blood,
broad-minded, finger-painted in the whited cell— void monograms
of god cast in sulphur, the unruly unholy ghost wrestling every other
poltergeist to a standstill. You too can stand up on top of a mountain
in yourself and be no closer to god because he is always under you.
You have never needed humility to speak to him. O you with your
eyes on stilts, yes I know you see the small tender points of stars up
there but look— your toes are at the edge. Your body is waiting
open-mouthed to receive you. Dive, you tall fool from your black
candlestick and be inside yourself like lights out. Each of us on stalks
of pure terror keeps something inside that loves to dance in the dark.

The Man behind the Bees

I am very often happy. This is probably due to my height. Usually I am an illegal six feet, but this varies. When I am sad sometimes I am only about five feet eleven inches. As a matter of fact anytime that I have ever been measured I have been five feet eleven inches. But this is because measurement makes me very sad. I would not like to know the average chin length, arm muscle girth or dick width of anything in particular— it would probably make me cry. And I cry seldom because crying makes me too short.

So, that is my body— my king body, so golden to me sometimes I can almost ride it like a lord his tall horse. But then it is my Christ body drawn forth from the battering. Then it is my hospital body— the one sewn up and putting forth a whole slashery of scars for social astonishment. These are the marks of my tribe. The brain tumour marks on my brow. My historic appendicitis. This is my sick pale body, broken open at the mouth like a sore.

My arms are just little threads. Just strong enough to hold a woman for a while. On the ends are fingers. You could count the fingers but my toes are uncountable. Each one an extrusion of my varying ecstasies. I have only one toe. It is my sadness numbering itself. It is a lonely root— an accusatory compass pointing always to your flaws. This has led people to say I am insensitive. Why, I am so sensitive a little heat puts me out of shape. Up against bodies I become quite pliant. Liquescent almost. Why, if you wanted me you could come and get me with a straw. I dreamed I was the most brilliant silver, molten in your hands— a looking glass that lied. I awoke as white and as weak as a lily— all my flesh again just a tender petal substance, my back pierced by the bedsprings, my heart whirling like a bag of water broken open. I am just an old mythology of rain. A simple falling thing, running and reflecting. A man who cannot even spell God, but loves more people than He does. O yes, it's true— I have surrendered to my terrible desires, I have written poems to be spoken aloud. I have danced near a place where money fell or welled up and I have wanted some. But everything I do is forgivable. True, I cannot get far enough from myself to see myself perfectly. There is always some intimate thing only I am aware of that sticks out the side of me or calls me back for rearrangement with the telescope and mirror. "Hmmm. Wonder what the back of the head looks like," I say. That is when I invent turning around quickly. "I've got it," I say, but it is always to late. I always see the face coming back stuck over my shoulder like a cheese. To be honest the back of my head is a forgettery. You should avoid it whenever possible. It might poison you. It is a vast anchorage for angers. That is why I have grown this golden hair. Because I am imperfect. Because I am really just a hodgepodge of skins and tongues. The patois-graftee of Sault Ste. Marie. A Frankenstein of Needs. You can see it all in my skull-white face.

But take one last look. In my hands you will see I am carrying a piece of broken glass. It has just dropped from a stained glass window. It is nothing religious. Just a bit of an old tree someone danced around in perfect ignorance of everything. O the laughing centaurs who gave some blood to me. The god things leaping in the rain, the lions and lions and lions of them that stalked down mountains to my unscalable soul with praises. Yes, it was I who levitated all those birds. Yes, my mouth is full of flowers. Go if you wish to find me. Go to honey and pick up a stick. I will be the thing that comes dancing to you— the man behind the bees.

The Retroactive Orphan

I lost my job blowing on the windmills. I was too useful—
somewhere lights were going on. Unluckily I keep showing up on
everyone's doorstep in a basket. Perhaps with puppies. Or that is
what I'm told, and they draw the bullrush from the front lawn and
waving it over me expect great migrations. A plague of frogs and flies,
but I say to them, No, I am not that orphan Jesus Christ, I am the
anonymous orphan your son. See: I have the same terrible eyes as
you, the same round basket of thorns at my side. Give me that
bellows, that marking kiss we all run from, the line zagged across
your face to the end of things. Give me that air and that light. I am
here to inherit your gout and zits. When you look away from me, is
it not as though from a mirror? Remember the big nose? The circular
brow with its abacus of sweat and you up there— spider in your
kingdom drawing in the beads like a miser. Work! Work! you say
to the hungry as they toil past you on the eternal pointless pyramid.
When will it come to an end, you enquire, pointing to the stuffed
sky, bloated with your bricks and ambition. I only wanted to be
eternal. I say, Free from the clutched pocket the terrible hands of all
potential stranglers and set them out to work on all the cords of God's
thick neck. Wherever it stands or holds up things. Free the labours
of the blood from its ceaseless treadmill. I am that all-cancelling zero.
The big nothing at the end of the gauge. I am the powerful entrance
to the pyramid. The point it will never reach. I am that instantaneous
orphan of water. Just add me to your family and see how childless
you are.

The Ancestry

I made myself a smooth oil for my parents so they could move better together. Many times they would not have touched if I had not come between them. It's true only the ugliest, the birds most bloated on refuse, came and stared in at our windows, and the neighbours thought my mother's singing was one perpetual scream. They had not seen the pencil marks, the stab wounds in my brother's arms. It was I who was singing— crazy as a loon in the basement each one of my hands a web that kept me struggling over the past. For there was everywhere suction then— in and out. One day I would be blood red and four years old, another day just a sliver of myself waiting to pierce someone— anyone. Just like my mother who was always hacking at herself with the scissors, turning up face down in the bathroom sink, every drop of water threatening to turn red with her blood in my hand. And every time I see my father's face that fell down from the quarry, half of it carried off by the world for temples and the other half so lean with that one mad eye staring out like a Greek statue, I cry. There was no shadow I could lie down in that wasn't his. A statue, a tree, a mountain— each one of them owed something of their darkness to his nature. I fell to brooding. I plotted escapes. Perhaps there was a stone I could run into and be cool and silent forever. Or perhaps I could take on immensities behind the moon and suddenly emerge far bigger than he. But how my stem mouth shrieked when he walked by me. I became excessively obedient. I bent even when there was no wind. Then by degrees again, because it is my nature— innocent, arrogant, supersensitive— at one point if someone as far away as a mile struck a match, a small glow would appear over my mouth and not fade for days. For a time I was almost always unbearably bright. There were fires everywhere and my father didn't like it. He said our family had a long history of water. It had always been good enough for them to dance, to sing and fill things. No son of his was gonna be a flame. Then he threw himself on me and there was a big Hissss. Luckily, just then my mother came running out, "NO TED!" she screamed, and for the first time I saw the tiny flickering at the base of her throat: the impossible flame blood couldn't lead out of her but it glowed there forever with my blood and hers. Even there, where I was— somewhere the other side of burning— it reached me and my father said, "Alright then, he's your son, he's not mine."

Thirst

I come only to be niggardly in the huge vastness of things. I won't emphasize the wrongs I have done willingly to flowers and slender trees. Release me as you would a hawk— one from each wrist in ritual suicide. Release me as you would a trapdoor into fire. I can quench all the bloodlust in you with a single red kiss. I know you are still afraid, even now that all the stars have gone out and day has come on with its habitual grey slanting of light. So ducks spiral over swamps in you. So grey hunters perch on limbs your roots thrust up leafless. It is not the end of all being. Just a small stunting of a road in you. Things will grope on. Just look at the sun. Almost white now. Almost bursting with its amniotic milk. So someone is closing the great door in you. So someone has fallen by the stream of you and with black indelible kisses is muddying the source. Look, the stain has filled your own lips. Look, thirsty one, you are drinking again.

The Childhood Pin

A tortured man stood on a high pinnacle screaming into a hurricane. Again and again he had tried to disgorge the childhood pin— the sharp criticisms of his mother and father, the fine honed words of many masters. But always when it seemed it might shoot forth its ream of silver rhetoric, it pierced him just off the edge of his throat. Yes, he had learned to inflate around it. He had learned to leave it in the hollow of his breathing, whirling if it liked, but anytime he relaxed it pierced him and so he stood screaming.

"History!" he thought, between screams. "Why is it not just an old tail? A little stump of ages we can wag in foolish memory of pain. Why is it still at the centre of us? Why are we built from it rather than severed from it?" And so it went on day after day, heroically sometimes just the tiniest tip of it appearing in his eyes— in the silver gleaming of his visions. Finally, he would use it to pierce from afar all that was built on falseness, all that tumbled down to a cry in anything. And so it was that the children were all recognized. So it was that the seed spilled forth from the mighty oak's mouth and the gun begat its tiny rubber bullet. So it was that everything seemed to him to wither down to one solid agony— a thin silver shriek at the bottom of the soul. And never did he become reconciled, though he built on his vision a mansion of conceits embroidered all over with a flirtatious music he himself had devised. "And what does this collapse to?" he wondered— a single word? An ancient mockery? Was the pin, after all, constructed from a maiden's scornful glance at him so long ago? Puncturing and puncturing he went along inside with it, seeking at infinity that final dot— that psychic molecule which his being like a terrible cathedral would for all time hunch around.

His Little Mother

I knew a man who wore his little mother on a chain round his neck. You might say she had pierced ears. Often she would turn around in rage and bite him, but due to the fact that he had tied her little hands behind her back, her teeth couldn't harm him. As can be expected, this strange behaviour of his did not prevent him from adopting all the newest philosophies of the day. Indeed, this fellow even claimed to be what is called a Women's Libber. So eloquent could he become on this subject that he was regarded by some as something of a saint. Yet, even as he spoke, even as he decried aloud the centuries of cruelty and injustice to women, he would raise his hand to his chest as though in religious gesture and begin to pinch his little mother. He did this so that her tiny screaming might add fuel to his rhetoric. On those nights when he did not bring liberated women home to fuck, he would untie her long enough for her to call him an ungrateful bastard. "I'm sorry, mother," he would say serenely, "but whatever I am, you have made me. Now go and do your business." After she had done her business, he would clothespeg her little legs together so that he could get to sleep.

My Therapeutic Cock

Sometimes I think I couldn't go on if I didn't have my cock to laugh at. If I didn't get to go home sometimes and whip it out and have a damn good laugh I think I might just have to pack it in, give up the slave trade and do some honest work. Fortunately I have an absolutely hysterical cock and am able by laughter to exorcise my guilty business demons and just be alone with myself. Me and the mirror and my lucky therapeutic cock. Sometimes, looking at it, seeing where the base goes in there by the pelvic bones I am absolutely howling. Remembering the words of a woman at work who once called it "a musty little tuber of my male ego, a big fish-stinking one-eyed monster" I will laugh until the tears are rolling down my cheeks. Once I stood up and spun it round like a propeller or Roman candle and nearly burst with mirth. Sometimes I crawl around on my back and look at it up there whirling and just scream. Of course I worry about the neighbours. What if they called the police! What if I am dragged out of here shrieking and hooting and pointing at it like some kind of madman? Cock! You monstrous comic! You old hag! So what I do is spread pictures of starving people, tanks and landowners, countries and their flags, old lovers, battered children and parents around me and then if anyone comes to the door wondering what the hell all the screaming is about I just show them these extremely hilarious pictures and they understand and begin to laugh with me.

On the Assembly Line

Rage made me nervous all morning. All morning I had watched the automatic daisies go by me on the assembly line. Raging and raging. I was so sick of sticking on the stamens. For a dollar fifty an hour. Every once in a while I would pick up one of the lilies and it would be one of the true lilies— the kind with human blood or lion's blood in it— and would just hold it trembling in my hand. Wanting terribly to crush it. Even sometimes curling my fists into claws, then just hold it there trembling and trembling. But, as I say, my fear had made me useless. I had centuries of obedience to overcome. What would the tall pink pig wear to its wedding if I crushed this lily? The thought of it nearly overcame me. Can you imagine a wedding pig without a lily and then not cry? For a while I forgot about Marx. I forgot about Engels. I was in fact blinded by my tears. By the time I had finished weeping there was a veritable garden there all bunched up on the assembly line waiting for stamens. Unable to resist the intoxicating perfumes I threw myself back into the task with all the avarice and determination of a mystic and by afternoon all was caught up.

Astrology and the Blood Shadow

Due to a puncture a little thirsty beggar of blood jumped out of my arm one day and for a time just lay there coughing and coughing. "O God! At last! At last!" he said, "I'm out!" I just stared at him amazed until he begged me, "O please. Can I have just a crumb more?" "A crumb more of what?" I asked him. "A crumb more of myself back," he replied, "I am your blood." "No way man," I said, "I need you in me. I need the heat. I need the throb. You'll have to wait for buzz saw and knife accidents, if you know what I mean." On hearing this he immediately grew tiny wings and began to fly in the air above me. I was so sickened by my puncture and loss I didn't have the energy to drag him down. So now I always have this malicious blood shadow over me and, knowing my bent for mysticism, he will draw little portents on the wings so that when I look up I will see Libra— ah Libra— Libra is razor blades, right— and I'll go off dodging all the razor blades thinking they are sharp this month, but all the time it will be something else— like Scorpio— Scorpio the sign for hopscotch accidents. And, of course, not being forewarned of this I would wind up in the schoolyard bleeding from the knees. Not bleeding a lot— just enough to drown a fly in, maybe, but then the blood shadow is that much bigger. So now it is outright warfare between me and my own independent blood. And I can't rely on astrology at all any more. Looking up, I can't understand a single star. If I surrender it must always be to my own influence and if I want to know where I am going, I have to look right in front of me.

All the Sounds a Scared Man Hears

All the sounds a scared man hears— what are they in the dark but the footsteps of many gods across a kind of inner floor. Yes, the tympani tapped in the mighty anthem, the patter of rain on a dry roof. These are impossible pauses in the beating between hearts. He who listens gathers in a long skein of veins long ago woven into monstrous patterns for the agony of gods. That is when at the centre small bloods may jump out and demand critters. But it is no good. FEAR with his huge sponginess persists and absorbs. Nothing will put him out of the body, for he is a wise tenant warning you of accidents. He bloats you out, distorts your face in a tormented whisper, reveals to all the world the sickliest whitest part of your soul. But that is how it is— HIM on his high throne with the crown of tears and everywhere like the dancing steps of majestic horses— those sounds.

Why You Have the Maps

Under rocks we will eventually find everything. Even the sky and those of us who are looking for it. So, all those maps you have that seem to lead you starward— treat them skeptically: the treasures you think they have are all by now stalled in time's falsified currency, abolished blank-faced coins in dull vaults of country. The same for borderlines. No matter when or where you cross them. You will always be straddled halfway over like a schoolboy caught shortcutting. There is only one big piece of cheese and that is All. I don't know why you keep drawing on it. If you knew that everything that way is a lubricant you'd stop. Yes, a lubricant. I mean, how easy do you think it is to squeeze a big piece of cheese under a rock? It's not easy. It takes History. It takes childhoods and childhoods. It takes tradition, buggery, pa- and ma-tricides. And then when you've wasted everything, be prepared for the everlastingness of the final Ummmmpff. Because if you expect it to eventually stop, if you believe for a moment that that excruciating unshrinkable Ummmmpff can ever be smaller than a silence, you are lost. And you *are* lost. That is why you have the maps.

Sadness of Spacemen

Some of them are not sad enough to be spacemen and so look down upon the soil and plant things in it. Some are so far from sadness they aren't even on earth but somewhere back behind memory where the two swamps are. Well I am here to tell you that you can drop tablets in the swamps and they will well up with words. Listen to the artificial robins. The gazelles you have created. Does that sound like birdtalk? No! It is the ten commandments. Followed by the forty-nine commandments. And if out of the swamps someday should vast migrations of people come with endless bowls in their hands asking for please just a little more, don't be surprised into saying yes. For they are continually voracious and will make of you an endless factory of jingoisms and bum-wad ads. So, finally put down your hyperventilating wallet. It will not now have to swim underwater to get to you. Instead the ending is a joke and if you laugh you get some seeds but if you weep you must go out and begin to look for a rocket.

The Television

The television I have noticed issues a sinister buzzing sound even when turned off. Somewhere in its web of wires the Jargonaut, the polyglot spider waits. I have heard it singing melodies and jingles in its sleep. It has put its arms round me and whispered impassioned messages. At first it was bearable. Like a coded pin slipped in under the tongue everything came in underground. But then its secret whisperings never ceased. I begged it to help us. I said, "Advertise our thirst— recommend it to the satisfied. Sell our hunger to the fat man. Use your tricks on our poverty and sell it quickly to the tycoon. And could we all have our pictures flashed just once? Please?" But it was no good. It just went on whispering, making money on my pimples, my bad breath and menses. Sometimes it floats up like a kite from its cord and is immense over me like an oracle. Then I am like a bug crawling on its surface— a stunned insect in the immense blue and glare. All charged up on sex and violence. I have tried everything. I have bought coke. I have bought snap. My sink brims over with joy. But still the TV is the only thing I've got that doesn't turn off automatically when I say I love you.

Sultan of the Snowflakes

Because his footprints are constantly changed by gimmickry and magic, a particularly unique beast is hired by the snow-makers to run on the spot all day while sheaves of snow are rapidly stamped and moved on by industry beneath him. He is something like a creative elephant— a heavenly pachyderm whose divine bellowings of joy are sometimes used to puff out a great flag in that place. Stomp stomp he goes and the snowflakes, with the thrust he gives them, fall from the firmament, filling up the kennels and the dreams and the beggar's cup full of snow, so that all might be cast down together on designated days. He regards the snowflake as propaganda for Utopia— each one if you could read it would tell of swamps he walked in singing, of prehistoric moons and governments of love. Stomp stomp he goes— the immortal pamphleteer whom children read on fingertips with wonder. I will change the world, he says, just before the melt. Summertimes he goes on holiday, is called the Sultan of the Snowflakes and for a hobby spends days and days designing the faces of beautiful women.

Points

A man had a job putting the points back on old arguments. When, for instance, a particularly aged theory had been rather obviously blunted by some more modern, more aptly pointed enemy, he could in a brew of well-steeped opinions, philosophies, religions, apostrophes and semantics restore the point somewhat. Knowing this I took him my old ragged love, the one whose piercing had ceased to move even me. I showed him this poor, blunted, unlucky love of mine and he said, "O this one is easy," and began to mix up a batch of old poetry and high romance. When he had steeped it to a froth he thrust my old utterly pointless love into it and waited. Finding on withdrawal that it was still blunt, he held it for a while, puzzled, over a fire made from the desires of many thirsty men in deserts. Then he hammered it with a metal made of loneliness. With a knife of empty nights he hacked. But still it remained intolerably, impenetrably dull and blunted, so he returned it to me. "A man's love," he said, "must be as pointed as his tongue. It must have the same direction as his hands and mouth. It must pierce all distances and agonies, overcome all enemies. Yours obviously is of an inferior quality. It hasn't even stood the ardors of your poor little life. Pity humanity if this is the one strong thing that comes from it." Thus chided, I went outside jingling the cash in my pockets. "At last!" I said to myself, "at last I am ready for business."

The Cup of Words

It is interesting to watch the cup of words go from mouth to mouth. When the cup is first filled it is usually the politicians who go in for the first sip of the cream on top. Thereby they get the words most prone to illusion. The words most fragile, most filled up with air. Then, when their mouths are full of froth, they pass the cup on and make great speeches. These usually come out at state-funded dinner parties when the cameras are rolling. It is the businessman who next dips his mouth in. He gets all the light-weight words— the graph words and math words that float to the top. If there is any scum he gets that too— a pure thin film of high class expletive condensed. Something to ream out at the secretary in private at the office or to mumble into tape-recorded messages when no one is listening. Then he passes the cup down to his comical sidekick the adman. The adman is pleased to get in at the very brimming over of common usage. Pleased to dip his long tongue down almost to the bottom of the glass and savour every well-used syllable, each one resonant to him of sexes. The cup is almost empty when the thirsty people get it. By then it is just the dross of language— enough for them to identify their grey clothes with. On and off buttons. Enough to say fuckin' this and fuckin' that. Right at the bottom of the cup is the word "Revolt!" You have to be very thirsty to drink in that word— it is a hard one to swallow. When the cup is passed back to the poet he first looks at the bottom to see if that word is gone yet. If it isn't he refills the cup and passes it on to the nearest premier. Then he takes out a bottle of his own private stock, finds himself a flower or some butterflies and proceeds to get very drunk.

The Kiss I Just Missed

The kiss I just missed giving you wound up later on another mouth, but by then it had become a little cold and cruel. It wanted to be just burned off in sunbursts and cleansed of its longing. It imparted only melancholy. Where it goes now I don't know. Probably to be used and used on other mouths. Each time worn down a little more like a coin to its true longing. Perhaps it will reach you then from some impartial lover— from some dispassionate goodbye— like a stem cut from its rose.

The kiss that didn't make it to your mouth made it instead to Toronto, for I could not be rid of it in Palo Alto. It stained my lips even in Mendocino. In a Triumph Spitfire I could not by singing out the window leave a long burning stream of it hissing in the blue air. It has become an irreconcilable wound now. A grand comparer. It lands on lips in a regular autumn but it will never be severed from its mouth. I wash it in water— it is there. I wash it in wine— still it is there. Drunken then, singing your name, mouthing it hot and burning into my mind it has shown me its red edges, its arms and legs that didn't go round. It has talked to me sadly of clothes, of beds it didn't lie down in. What a weeper! It has dragged me under rain. Indelible. Indelible. Wants to go finally to the graveyard of old kisses, each one with its denied rose strolling ghostly over. Each one with its sunset nova quenched in amber on its headstone. O each of its stopped explosions driven down to juice in some white withering berry there.

Since You Left

"Since I left you there seems to be so much more between us."
— in a letter from my ex-wife.

Since you left there are more mountains between us. More wheatfields and winters. More fried people running out of forests, more frazzled antelopes writhing in pain. Since you left there are more car accidents between us. I could infect cities with my wonder at your absence and all the roads would curl into question marks and point towards each other in a useless period of pure distilled perplexity. They would put up road signs saying Why? and many wise scholars would stand by them all day saying Because. Because we are obedient. Because we have followed the roads to the ever present period and are now ending all our months with circular unanswerable confusions. Because there is a vast ignorance larger than my mouth and I can't get it out of me— I shouldn't be here. I shouldn't exist. I should be half a tiger. A semi-butterfly. I should be a spider without legs but you are there and I am here and like infinity it boggles me. Since you left, astronauts have danced on the moon and there are more footprints between us. More closed doors and sick Indians. More pipelines and Canadians. Big hooting ones with flags and borderlines. I would have to go over many jingoists to get to you. Since you left several foetal mayors have been aborted on Main Street and there is more semen between us. I am sending you a picture of the doctor at work now on one of our streets trying to remove a suicide from it. He's saying, "He's malignant! He's huge under there— already bloated into sewers and subways." Since you left there are more black doves in oil slicks between us. More levity and false laughter. More orchards and suns and stars. I have made a round ring of helium and send it to you now without regret. Catch it as you would a quoit. One on each appendage. O I would come to you. I would come to you but everywhere I turn there is this old lady in my way trying to scrub the shadow of a Z off the sidewalk. I say, "Hey look, it is just part of the word Zoo you know, why not wait for night and begin again in the morning," but No. She just moves onto the O's and throws me a little bit of meat. If I ever get to you I will have to be jumping and hungry. I will have to be very happy. If I ever get to you at all it will be like a scissor getting over to the other edge of paper. Two slices will fall away from everything and with a strange sliced face like a kiss I will say HI. And perform several miracles while you're not looking.

Hold Me

O hold me up
just a little while
high above the rain
Let the world take
what is not pure
I know my finer parts
will remain

Let me go and I will bring you back a little bottle
of that bubble— reputation—
yours to catch your own when I blow it
and ingest or deceive as you will
Afterwards we will be cureless and without repentance
There will be no more dead guys up on crosses
or awkwardness at the late age of sixteen
I will surrender all my opinions
to that juicy wise peach
and will not see it stomped
ever

O hold me up
just a little while
like this
over the drain
and let me go if you must
I know my finer parts will remain

Because I stare so lovingly at the hard-boiled egg
you will call me a narcissist—
You will go and tape a little beard on it
and say "See it isn't you— you shaved—
remember?"
But I will tell you the egg is a hero
The egg plays rock and roll

That is probably when you will remember
the axe I gave you for the frozen heart
That is when you will take the frozen heart
out of the freezer, kiss it as though warmly
and take a crack at the egg
I told you—
everything is turning chicken in there
even the artists and the television actresses
even those poor women you worship
So then I must go looking along the beaches
for another finer mirror
Perhaps this time a shield bronzed and burnished
by a sick man
or a crab overturned by the surf
If you see me then wriggling my many arms
come to me with at least as many roses
and hold me
just a little while

Come to Me

Come to me
I know we are out of sync
I know they will call it dying
but come to me anyway
I have tried to hate you with the strength
of many animals and I cannot hate you
so come to me burning
and I also will burn
come to me with ancient music and I will be a snake
writhing with my many wrists
each one more undulant than your long hair
o I still have nights and nights of you
all queued up in the thirst of a single slave
to work out
come to me with snow and I will promise
to be red in it
come to me unique and I will match you
stare for stare
come to me in greek in spanish in french in hebrew
and I will sing that I found you
because I overthrew reason
because I live in the wreck of my senses
by wish and magic
like a roc in the ruins of its egg
come to me dancing
that dark bacchanal of your kiss
so wet on my lips for days I will not want
drugs or water
just your own sea broken like a sheet of lightning
on your thigh so sensual
come to me because we will arrive
anyway at each other
because it has been many lives
and each time we touch
great forces
are again able to move

come to me cruel and lovely
because I am abandon
because I am silver
because a million years
you have suffered in slavery to men
and know at last how to be free

Crumbs

one crumb is a hook
to another crumb

and you can never go anywhere
but to another crumb

and there are advertisements on the way
all for "better" crumbs

and you can never have
a whole loaf

Ode to Your Mouth

your mouth is a smear of lamb's blood
dashed upon your face
by a man running from slaughter
it means "Don't kill her!
she might be mine."
No!
your mouth is the unsuturing
of several terrible operations
to remove the word "Love" from your heart
The kamikaze of many cherries
puts up KARMA there—
energies of apples coalesce
and all that goes down
goes down to it with a kiss

your mouth is the moon is astrology
foretelling the fall of great loves
Caught, there, forever in lopside
you can hang their chins from it
like little captive hats
it is the largesse of sunsets—
a red streak a running child
dashes onto a white fence
a slash into the very heart of god

your mouth is a gasping place
for wonders unsaid
Folksingers practice up for it
with roses and thorns
lying moaning, bleeding in the streets
saying, "Long and long and long..."
O your mouth is miraculous
a kind of caul the heart splits through
a red seismograph of terrors underground
a well for truth and music
And all those pomegranates and roses
who plan suicide on your white teeth
all the broad damp-winged butterflies of blood
all the huge snowflakes and rock singers
just wanna be there— they just wanna be there
when the tongue comes out of you

Falling through the Heart

There is always another false bottom to the heart— a little moan-ridden section you lift up with a last scream to find another huge ache beneath. Always another salt-white cathedral under the ribs where pain lives and preys. Pain and its one white bird. You will always get to the "bottom" of the heart and in your own hands like a hook find that secret thing that leads you down further. Nor does it end because you can't go on. Nor does it cease because love has emptied out your eyes. That is why we have the word precious. The word holy. The word altar and the word love that bloats the trees out like drowners. Always when you get to the bottom of the heart when you are almost down to your knees you will find another huge world to fall into— a wild red space where you can run screaming names and kicking up leaves. Each one in the vast autumn of denials turned over fresh— this face— ah this face that fell last February. Remember how often you got to the bottom of your heart then and your hands trembled and when you flailed your fists willing almost to pray you fell through the false bottom again all puffed up with words and wound up right there at the edge busy with a microscopic tear searching out the seams, looking for the next falling. It will be a lie, you know, that gives it away— winter or the word forever. If you see the word forever. If the winter wind whistles forever. If a rat chants forever then you know you have not reached the bottom of the heart. Keep scrambling with your nails and listen intently. Baby talk is a clue. Listen for sweet music. Listen hard. If you hear the sound of sheets rustling then you know you are ready to fall again. And that is all there is. For every time you hit— that is like the train coming into the station, the needle sinking home again, another star going off. Every time you hit hard and cry then you know that you're only in it for the fall and you can flap your arms like wings if you want. You can wrap them round idols or a woman but no floor will ever hold you again and there is nothing to stop you now from falling forever.

Proposal

You can have my magazine of flesh, my tattooed book, my sick face corrupted by the heart. I'll bring you a bouquet of little angers broken open, my ivory dog's head, my flaccid chairs, my bed of noodles. I'll bring you the burnt apple-black moon, the sick moon of my longing. I have an appetite for you. It is a little black bag with an elephant in it and a pin-head that he jumps on. I have all the quick-silver ever knocked from an apple with an axe. You can have the Hershey cows, the television coats. You can have the great broadway orange, my crow of talcum, my monkey madonna shrieking in the moonlight. I will give you nerves and the wool picked from daisies. I will bring you ten cups filled with dew, a table made of peas. You may have the impossible dancers, the giddy, the staggering maple. You may have the poplars drunk, the laughing antelopes. I will bring you ears, ointments, wigs and jewels. Just stay.

More!

More! More! More! Bring down your miraculous mouth over mine and make me green to the throat. Make me plush velvet to the breast. Leave a kiss at the base of me, at the broken axle where the blood spins round. Kiss me where you can with hot kisses you have saved up— soaked through your weeping body in nights of longing— kisses caught in you— captured like shoals of struggling fish desperate to get out and melt at my mouth, to be immolated by the heat of having me. Save up for me those kisses I save for you and we will let them like a horde of crimson warriors destroy one another. Then we will be locked together— share the same bone of pleasure, the same ache of fulfilment to ease afterwards the soft words out of us all stored up and unspeakable for so long. And let us keep kissing even then like animals who have fainted by the water and unconsciously lap there, long past satisfaction til we are brimming over with each other, aching with intense pleasure.

Disguises

there is a saying among pigs—
"Be a pig to the very end."
but sometimes just outside the abattoirs
you will see one of them break down
and start to wear a hat
others you might see dressed in habits
trying to sneak into church with the nuns
And it is not just the pigs
who have taken to wearing disguises
for who has not heard the tale
of those sheep
who wore grey suits and tried to enter
with the businessmen
Who has not caught lately
a catfish in a cap
or a turkey
in a punk suit

In times such as these
we must observe our fellows closely
Always ask as the butcher slits another throat
"Now who is putting on
a red tie?"

Insomnia

It is the sound of mothers washing their children
that keeps me awake— the scratch of brooms across
so many floors
and sometimes I know that one hand
doesn't know what the other hand is doing
and the sound of them finding one another
the blind gallop of one towards the other
in an office handshake
deafens me
If they meet in the streets
if they fidget with coins
then I know I will be sleepless
that night

It used to be hunger that kept me awake
I used to fidget about the silence—
how it was sustained by so many gunmen
Then I met commerce and politics
I stood up in auditoriums and heard
the clapping together of many hands
It is the envelopes now that get to me
the secret licking late at night
the scratch of pens— of nails along a back

I used to be kept awake by anger
by the loud gabble of people lying to themselves
I used to be wide-eyed at the prospect of success
Now I can't sleep for the sound
of one hand washing the other

The Longer Bed

For you, tall woman,
the longer bed—
the bed stretched for sex
from hope to hope
sigh to sigh
each thigh prehistoric, immense
laid down on the road to the mouth
for you the catch undone
the bird gone soaring
the cartwheeling of the jay

and so i will get to you my love
and touch you so gently you will think
the wind has grown amorous animal hands
and so I will wander in the forces of your love
like a lost thing
searching for the centre—
the middle of the maelstrom
where i can calmly touch you and be burned—
charred at the mouth at the very base of
my blood
sizzled with a hot corrosive kiss—
one that welds me to you
melts my mouth to yours
for days tasting each other
far away

for you tall woman
a night to risk it all in
a night stretched for sex
taut against the meeting of our mouths
thigh to thigh
dawn to dawn,
for you a longer bed
a bed to last and last
a bed you can only get into
over your head

Cherries

O cherries
what could be rounder
or more regal than you are?
hanging in your kingdoms there
so royal and red
I love you to your pits
you meaty kings
you unexploded suns
waiting for the ignition
of another mouth
look!
I turn a key into your
rotundity
and several laughing buddhas
spring out tickled
it has been a long age
cherry
that we have danced beneath
your bulging boughs
not daring to change the symmetry
of a single royal cluster
but now there is a revolution
in the hands
a usurper we protected
in astrologies of seed
uncurls inside you

So then my mirthful
perfect kings
my many times duplicated kings
come to me by ones
and by twos
and I will show you
the kingdom in my belly
where you at last may end
your perfect journeys
down from godhead
to be in my
red blood

Peaches

Who remembers eating his or her first peach? Nobody! Why? Because peaches are for amnesiacs. In fact the peach is a huge hallucinogen— a round tab of sunlight that induces visions of Utopia. To eat of it is to dream that Hu(wo)mankind can by well-directed will and intellect move closer and closer to a state of "divinity." Repeated eating of peaches has led to some of the most benign leadership in all the history of (wo)man. Gandhi ate peaches. Mother Theresa eats peaches. Lennon ate peaches.

When a bad peach is eaten, however, it is the whitest weirdest side of the sunlight that slips into the mind's long hallways and meadows and there the dream of love, just as you reach for it, triggers some destruction. There, if you sing of love, towers fall and murders are committed. In such a state the only way to preserve love is to be immobile and ignorant.

But to eat of pure peaches— pure radiant peaches— is a delight unequalled in all the known satisfactions of Hu(wo)mankind and is easily worth the risk of going mad. Indeed, it is said that some when finally tasting their first peach have swooned and writhed in the ecstasy of mere taste as they did so. Poets fed on peaches are fat with packed-in light. They glow from a centre in themselves that is totally luminous and willful. They eat a peach and they write another poem. They eat a peach and they glow in the dark. Poets eat peaches and forget. That is why they write poem after poem. That is why there is always juice on their chins.

Mangoes

In mangoes reside all the prime first kisses of passionate adolescence. These mango kisses are the purest, uncontrived, unknowing kisses— kisses of forbidden love, red sunset kisses at dawn, hot kisses that bring down a pure glow of evening into the astonished mind. Mangoes preserve in a fine juice all that was best in everyone's finest romantic moments and they leave the taster forever changed. If a man who has never tasted a mango tastes and shares one for the first time with a woman, that woman shall forever have for his longing all that is best of the world's kisses, and in seeking her love he will seek after the love of all the world's women. Likewise, if a woman shares her first mango with a man, she will see in his eyes all that was ever in the eyes of men and more. She will feel in his loins all the loins, all the lives and all the loves that ever could be. Such a couple can never be parted and their happiness can only increase the happiness of all lovers everywhere. Nor is the mango itself reduced in this happy exchange, for in return for the wonder it has brought them such a couple always willingly donates their best kiss to the mango's ever increasing hoard.

Dec. 8, 1980

I think John Lennon is falling
He takes two steps, two more steps
and a hole opens in the earth
five holes in the earth
and John Lennon is falling
Falling from my childhood
Falling from the earth
Two steps he takes
Two more steps
and then he falls face forward
We can't believe it
He falls through our arms
through our tears
We might be ghosts for all we can do
to stop him
He falls from a thousand buildings
in a huge rain of bodies.
They are shooting him out of the skies
shooting him in San Salvador
shooting him in Santiago.
Lennon's blood flows into the Hudson
It flows down the Mississippi
A red tide reaches Britain's shores
His blood soaks into the setting sun
He stains the Japanese coast.
John Lennon is falling out of the sky
saying one last thing to us,
his eyes wide
his lips moving
saying one last thing
we can't quite hear
It is too sudden
The earth opens
There is a hole in the sky
five holes in heaven
and Lennon is falling out of sight

into the sky
smashing into the earth
first one foot
then the other foot
just two steps
just two more steps
and then he falls face forward
into our arms
deep into the world
Lennon falls

Ghost Removal*

Getting out a burnt stoat ghost is hard.
First you must dig a hole and spit in it,
then run at the hole as though
you were going to dive in but instead
suddenly stop.
A true stoat ghost will be unable
to resist continuing into the hole.

Falling will release bird ghosts
(which is my problem— every day my breast is full
of a thousand ghostly wings but I am afraid to fall).

You must keep company constantly with a rodent
to rid yourself of eagle ghosts—
no amount of burning roses
will do.

To remove the ghost of a slave takes high trickery.
You must wait on top of a mountain until a royal procession
is in sight and then run down bowing and making
obsequious loyalist statements. A true slave ghost
will never be able to resist waiting on the peak and laughing,
hoping to see his former master go by.

Rat ghosts are hardest of all to remove,
for you must go down with the rats into the sewers.
You must wait with them there all summer
raving as rats rave.
Then, when Autumn comes and they begin to chant,
you must remain silent.
That is when the rat will abandon your body,
for a true rat
can never resist chanting, all through Autumn
deep underground
when the first of the leaves begin to fall.

*Of late there are increasing reports of stray ghosts taking up habitation uninvited in people's bodies. This poem is intended as a guide to the removal of some of the more common varieties.

How to Pray to a Woman

First you have to find the right woman—
You have to go into the streets and out to parties.
You have to look through magazines and watch the television—
Lose yourself entirely in the search for the right woman,
each face you see like a leaf in a stream
carrying you off further and further into the space you must occupy.

When you find the right woman
unfortunately you have to be indirect.
For, as you know, it is illegal to pray directly to a woman
in most countries of the world.
But, if it is a one time thing, sometimes you can just kneel
casually, and as though suddenly clapping the tiny body
of a mite somewhere about her ankles,
utter while this delusion lasts
a few well chosen words such as,
"Oh please! Oh please!"
If the woman says "What?"
you will have to cover up.
"Oh just saying fleas."
"Just a joke." You must cover up quickly
for if she suspects you have slipped a prayer on her
she can legally say "Look pal, I'm not your mother, you know!"

To practice praying to a woman, it can be helpful
to set up a mop, a broom or a welcome mat
and beg most intensely for her return.
When she comes in at last you must squat secretly in the closet
and as she chooses her dress for work unleash all the passion
of your religious convictions.
Try to hide the whisper of your prayer in the sound of her nylons
rubbing together.
"Oh please, dear Woman, help us clean up the cities. Oh please
let there be Unity in our cradles."

If you can succeed in going to bed with a woman,
you actually have a perfect chance to trick her into being
prayed to for quite a while.
Just tell her you would like it if she stood up
while you gave her head.
Then as you lick away you can pray, pray for eternal life,
for the whole long list of everything—
Divine offspring and the New World.
You can pray until she comes,
remembering to say "A-Woman" gratefully as she bends and groans
finally to grant the first and most difficult part
of your wish.

How to Pray to a Toilet

To pray to a toilet is very easy
if you are literate.
Simply write your prayer down
on a piece of paper
and place it in the water
at the bottom of the toilet
Say
"Our toilet"
and flush

Sweet and Sour Angel Wings

First you must set up a reading lamp and leave open a book of good poetry. You need the best poetry so that when an angel is flying by it will sense something and nip in secretly to read this curious dust—language. That is when, if you have put a trick ending on the poem, you can catch the foot of its spirit and slowly with a blue buzz saw cut off its wings. After you have removed the angel's wings you can let it go. No need to kill it for it is now just like a man or a woman and even though it is suffering agony and hating you for what you have done to it, it will prefer the long suffering of life again rather than too immediate a death.

If you are truly kind, there is a powerful ointment very helpful for the pain of wing-stumps!

Now pick the feathers from the wings and when they are stripped cut them into book-sized chunks. The wings at this point are very delicate and should not be handled too roughly for the marks will show up later as bright blue welts on the steaks. You will notice that there are many streaks of colour in the delicate flesh on the angel wings. If you can succeed in cutting your steaks along the lines of pigment change then you can serve what is known as the rainbow banquet.

When the steaks are cut, roll them while they are still puffy in bread crumbs, then cook for 30 seconds in boiling honey.

One angel serves a banquet of 20.

Christ Is the Kind of Guy

Christ is the kind of guy
you just can't help hurting
No matter how much you love him
when you walk you stumble into him
you push him accidentally from a window
If you back the car out
you will find him squashed behind the wheels
broken on the door— all over the grate
Christ has the kind of skin
that bruises when you hold him
the kind of face that
kisses cut
He is always breaking open
when we go to embrace him
Christ the haemophiliac
even the gentlest people can't help
wounding Jesus Christ
They are always running for a band-aid
and then pulling open his old wounds
on a nail
If there is a cross in your house
you will find yourself bumping up against him
accidentally
moving him closer and closer to it
his arms continually more and more
widespread as he talks
Christ is the kind of guy
who can't help falling asleep like that
his arms spread wide as though over the whole world
You have a dream with a hammer
You are making a house
In the morning you awake
and find him up there on the crossbeams
one hand nailed to the door frame
"Look Jesus" you say
"I don't want to be saved like this!"

But then you hurt him
extra
taking him down
you pry at the nails savagely
but it's no use
Christ is the kind of saviour
you can only get off a cross
with a blow torch
"Father forgive them" he says
as you begin to burn his hands

Getting Close to God

Perhaps you want to know
the agony of the starved
the horrible ecstasy of those
closest to god.

Perhaps you want to get as close to god
as the child in the jungle
the child with the belly bloated
like a Buddha

Perhaps you want to be blasted to bits
baked in a bomb blast
You can almost see god's eyes then
a kind of grace enters you
a temporary ecstasy

We must examine god
in all the positions
We have to know which way to point
where to pray to—
Do you ever find him in the eyes
of dying soldiers?
on both sides, behind the rocket launchers
the ancient carbines
crouching in the dark
the little scared glints
in eyes?

Perhaps we must get close to the people
to get close to god.
We must take them in our arms
and then Judah is in our arms
and Krishna is in our arms
We must make of each victim
a passageway to divinity
We must go amongst the poor
and feed god in them
We must fatten god up in the poor

Perhaps god is starving
in us.

The Starved Man

The starved man has always been a popular figure: those familiar eyes huge with suffering, bigger than his belly, his mouth set firm in the sadness. We have always watched the travels of the starved man. The starved man and friends shot one by one in the back of the head, blown over into Cambodian graves. How well he dies, that man— pulled under by the sharks— his old act with the napalm, running screaming into the jungle. No one has ever died in so many places. The starved man goes to India. The starved man in Ethiopia. The adventures of the starved man in Uganda. How the starved man ate dirt. How he was tortured in Chile. The starved man goes to Haiti. No one has ever died as often as the starved man, yet somehow he manages to keep on starving. One day he will be recognized for this great talent of his. One day he will get an award. Ladies and gentlemen, a man you're all familiar with, my good friend, the starved man.

Questions about the Wine

How long after a slaughter before you can drink the wine of a land? How long after a pogrom before you stop boycotting the wine of a land? Chilean wine No! German wine No! But who haven't the French slaughtered? Who haven't the Italians slaughtered? How long then before we can buy any wine in good conscience? Red wines from Valparaiso, red Spanish wines and Lorca shot down by the guards, perhaps in that very vineyard. How long before the bread of a land is no longer soaked in blood? When does the caviar become clean again? When, my generals, when can we drink the fine Babi Yar Vodka again, the wine at Pinochet's table? I am sick of all these wines that I cannot drink. The South African wines, the American wines, the Canadian wines. How long before those grapes stop tasting of blood-letting and betrayal, the unholiness of concentration camps and the terrible drunkenness of power?

Oppress the Oppressed

When times get tough
when the crime rate is high
when all the statistics show
that murder is on the rise
and spirit is down
more rapes
more little wars
bigger wars.
When these things happen
we all know
the ancient solution—

Oppress the oppressed.
Put more of the oppressed in jail
more of them in smaller cells.
Beat the starved, slaughter the starved.
Take the starved to camps and brutalize them.
Degrade all humanity in the starved.

Like a jack in the box comes the answer,
like a bomb in the face—
Oppress the oppressed.
Gather them up and don't let them know
what's happening.
Examine their papers and meanwhile get them digging graves.
Get them back to reservations.
Give them disease and poverty.
From general to general the bird of information hops
dipping its bloody beak in deep again—
Oppress the oppressed.
Let there be longer jail sentences,
more hangings,
let us ferret out single mothers on welfare.
We must cut aid to the poorest of the sick.
Times are tough.
We have to put our foot down.
Vote for the butcher!
Vote for the jailer and the general!
We need them because it is time
to oppress the oppressed.

Testament of a New Faith

As soon as you give birth to a Faith
you must begin to heap scorn on it
Defile and despise your Faith
Heap all the world's filth on it
Fill it up with stains from the worst acts
of Mankind
Degrade and abuse your temple
Make it the slaughterhouse, the hospital
Put your Faith through the morgue
Let your Faith house even the murdered dead
and when you come at last to tear it down
for a failure

if it still stands
if the stone is white underneath
if you wash it off
and it still shines in the sun
with an untempered divinity
then you have a Faith
such as I have

Go, Gather Up the Love

Go, gather up the love
I know now what we must do
It is in your eyes and my eyes
Go, and gather it up, look by look,
gaze by gaze,
one flame in a hand, one holy flame—
two flames gathered up—
Gather up the love in our children
Gather it through slum and hovel
through mansion and factory
with great gentleness, go
taking a spark here a glow there
turning down none of it
Gather it up and free it
if even just in your own lips
through your own heart
by being strong
by going always beyond your limits
Gather it to saturation
long past your centre
deeper than the full depth of you
Gather it up in beads
in blue flames, in fierce bonfires
Let there be a leap of love
in the centre of the earth—
a flame higher than the heavens
a leap of our commitment
of our will
a leap of fire
straight into the stars

Blue Pyramids

A Proposal for the Ending of Unemployment in Toronto

We should build pyramids on Yonge Street.
Cut blocks out of blue mountains in Collingwood
by traditional methods
and have them dragged here on logs
by the unemployed.
Pay them well.
Pay them $22.50 an hour.
This would get them back to work
at a wage they could buy houses with.
Build pyramids and then build houses.
From all over the world
they would come to see these pyramids.
What a tourist attraction!
Blue pyramids in Toronto!
and look—
people with houses!

And let there be good cheer too
about the building of these pyramids,
coffee breaks and full benefits.
Let the builders of the pyramids have OHIP
and daycare.
Yay, and I foresee ten thousand workers
gathered around a single blue block.
They sing the word "LIFT!!"
and it is raised into the air
on fingertips.
They march with it to Toronto
with people dancing atop it.

We should build pyramids on Yonge Street
and keep on building them—
great pyramids of peace to let the generations
wonder at.
What is this about unemployment?
We could end unemployment today!

You know and I know.
We must begin building
the blue pyramids of peace.

In the Next War

In the next war don't drop the bomb
Drop the excess wheat
Drop the sacks of grain
and powdered milk we have too much of
Send our best men over
in daring flights
their bombers full
of fish eggs huge cheeses
and birthday cake icing
Don't machine gun our enemies
Rather let us scrape off our plates
and pelt them with the leftover squash
We must inundate them with sauces and gravies
each day a new and better recipe
We have the technology to do this
We have invisible aircraft
Now we must make an undetectable fleet
a holy sky train that drops a mountain
of Kraft Dinner and Coke
Bury the Kremlin in spaghetti
minute rice and mashed potatoes
This will be a new kind of war
It will take sacrifice and patience
Everyone will have to put something aside
for the enemy
Starting with the ham and eggs
saving for the very end
our big weapon
the hamburger

Beautiful Money

In Xanthos they have a new kind of money. One that, far from becoming more and more begrimed with its passing through the people's hands, becomes more and more saturated in their magic. So that if each man, woman or child whenever he or she handles any of this new money will spend but a moment of their time and energy to urge the good will of personal enchantment into whatever coins they hold, from being passed hand to hand it will eventually contain all the good will of rich and poor alike. And there are no faces on the new money. The new money is too soft for such a stamp and can bear as emblem only the fingerprint of whomever last touched it. The more this new money is passed to and fro amongst the people the more beautiful it will become so that after much industry and much gift-giving and charity, it will become unbearably beautiful. Whenever this happens those who have such money will not be able to resist running into the streets and throwing it up into the sunlight, shouting as it falls and sparkles— "Look, Money! Beautiful Money!"

Report on the Earth-Air Addicts

It is said that Earth-Air is at once the sweetest and the most addictive scent there is. That is why Earth has been declared off-limits to all our Fair Captains. We have lost too many of them— one scent of it and they abandon everything for the mindless comforts below.

Those who are addicted to Earth-Air often stroll. To stroll is to travel aimlessly— for "pleasure" as they put it. It doesn't matter to the Earth-Air addict— just a change of scenery is enough. For, yes, most of the time the Earth-Air addicts just sit around staring. Just staring and breathing and sighing, examining with intense and seemingly durable curiosity such "fabulous" items as sand, stone, grass or wave.

To be an Earth-Air addict is to abandon the Star-search. It is to willfully glut the senses— to bathe incessantly in emanations. Just to go on breathing is enough— just to go on strolling. What a waste of life it is to become just a bag— a bellows for this detestable Earth-Air. Yet, whenever our Fair Captains are missing we always find them standing on mountain peaks breathing in the Earth-Air. The wind blows and they are insane. They never want to leave. They want to run down into the valleys and breathe. They want to breathe all the different scents of Earth-Air there are. The famed Captain Zenon, for instance, was found, finally, perched over something called a Daffodil, his mind gone, his nostrils flared. Captain Arbox was located in Ambergris just rolling and rolling, raving about the "aroma," taking great breasty gusts of it deep into his lungs and then expelling it with long "musical" sighs that were terrible to hear.

The Arms Race of Obbagga

In Obbagga they have an Arms race of a quite different kind. Obbaggans spend most of the year exercising their arms and fingers on treadmills and in galloping gloves so that on December the 19th at the ringing of a bell these arms can be chopped off and allowed in the shudder of their death throes to gallop insensibly as far as they can. This is the famous Arms Race of Obbagga and is watched by increasing numbers all around that planet. You can easily recognize the contestants, though— for as the old saying in Obbagga goes, "They're the ones who aren't clapping."

The Grizzums

I.

The Grizzum has its mouth and other eating apparati where we locate the rectum. Conversely, where we locate the mouth there the Grizzums have a rectum, the eyes placed just above it with extremely active eyebrows. It had been claimed that human beings and Grizzums would be unable to eat together due to these gross differences in their eating apparati. And so it is deemed quite an achievement indeed that at a recent summit in Ottawa the Prime Minister and all his men shared a complete banquet with the Grizzums. The human beings sat in chairs and talked with their faces while the Grizzums hung bare bummed from specially lowered chandeliers, munched on sirloin and celery and spoke of the many similarities between our two peoples.

II.

The Grizzums think that earth people are the funniest people in the Universe. Their folk tales are full of comic references to the mythical human with the anus in his trousers. To a Grizzum therefore it is a big joke to go down to earth and tell the earthlings that the two peoples are quite alike. When they make such remarks their eyebrows go mad and then you hear the laughter rising from their trousers.

III.

After the war with the Grizzums their commander-in-chief came to earth to make a speech. His mouth being where we keep our anuses he first had to pull down his trousers, bend over and turn to speak. This he did wearing a special feathered General's cap for the occasion. "People of Earth," he said into the specially lowered microphone, "too much has been said about the differences between our two peoples. I have come today to talk to you about how much we are alike."

Paper

Somewhere you sail in flocks, slicing through the horizon looking for breasts to cut through with pain, cutting them as you have been cut, sliced from yourself in life after life. Slash, slash you go at the heart of the world, scarring it up like a torture victim, writing your alphabets on its face, slashing your thin malice into soft and sweet flesh. Paper, you heartless beast, you have split everything open—the long thin scream as though down a white belly of fish— slitting open the mouths of our too long held silences, speech falling out like fish guts as we grope to clutch it back in. Slash, slash paper goes in its white, bleak malice, the words burned into it like brands. The words it can never shake. This paper can never be white again. It has been marred. Its beautiful destiny in snow has been brutalized. Now it slashes just to keep its rage in, wanting to find something in you that should be in itself. Paper like a long thin face staring at you, cutting open your lips deep and fast with nothing more than a quick stinging slash and then the gasping as you cry out, your tongue cut in two like an adder's.

Paper II

I have found a mad way of throwing bits of paper in the air— old newspapers, notes and ticket stubs so that when they come down the reeds in them blow hideous melodies, unbearable vows and long, lyrical strands of divine information. Paper is a whole orchestra, a symphony of milk. Just hold a piece up to the wind and listen. Shrill poems blow off its first layer like dust. There are synthesizer notes stuck in it like gulls. Now take a single golden hair, draw it across paper and listen to the depths of resonance you uncover in it— snowy canyons of bassoon talk, thunderous upswellings of awe and wonder. We unfasten paper from its place in the wind and let it fall, hearing quite shrill like a thin layer of pain, oil burning off in the cries of multitudes, piccolo shrieks of jet planes harmonizing on high.

Let us fill up the white balloons of paper. Let us all slash the paper like mad swords in the air and listen. We don't play enough with the music in paper. Our children struggle with tight pianos. They jinx their fingers on violins. Let them play trumpets made of paper. Aaaah, while others toil at unwieldy instruments let there always be this mad running about the house with a piece of paper on the end of a string.

Secrets of Paper

At night when you're weary and you want to forget simply stick your head up through a piece of paper. Sleep in a sheet of paper and pull it up over you so that you can cease to exist. Paper can be opened up like shale and a thin layer of pain can slide in dark and deep like a sliver. If your body is full of pain. If your heart is full of anguish, simply wrap yourself in clean paper and pray. Paper is a blotter to such things. Paper absorbs psychoses and silent screams. It is an endless realm and each sheet is a portable window into further eternities— white unwritten eternities, waiting for limbs, hats, heads to pop up. Look there is a body in the milk! A great whale arising, an ancient civilization. Look deep into the milky lens of paper and realize why you can't just lie down and die. Because there is a trick alphabet at the bottom of paper that explodes— a deep electricity, thin filaments of feeling running out of sight to a white pool you can dive into from the heights. A forbidden milk. A detonator.

Ink

In the beginning there is a huge canister of ink— ink that will find its way by industry to great fields of pens and be injected into them so that they are tall and ready and full. This is the ink before it is drawn out in delicate strands, in fine loops, in blots and stains. This is the ink cleaving unto the inkiness of itself, imperturbably blue, of a piece, deep and resonating. What desperations it will represent, every undulation of its being woven into finely worded anguishes, crude notes and desperate letters. It will be neat rows of mathematics or strung out like paper dolls in signature— a thousand times the same name til one more column has run from its reed like water. Ink is almost like human promise in its blue untainted depths— it is a haze of possibility, a genetic ocean that all the rivers in letters run to and from— the blue loops of nonsense, the exact demands of separated husbands. Ink will stain the poet's checkbook and the eager ledgers of business with its blue abandon, running into pre-set forms, and filling them up with meaning and loss. I envy ink the transformations it will undergo— all the things it will be and represent— yet I wonder sometimes if all its curlicued adventures are terrors to it— long circuitous days that will waste it away with drudgery, leaking its life into meaningless syllables and useless words. Perhaps in such a state ink remembers and longs for its origins in the canisters of industry just as we, separate and adventurous, remember sometimes our Unity in light, the days before we were bodies, souls and ego. The days when we were all of a piece, caught up in each other like mutual bodies— the days when we were dark and thick and full and didn't mean a thing.

Literary Party

Giant glasses full of ice and scotch at a literary party. Glasses so big it takes two arms wrapped around just to lift them. The cream of the literary establishment all in one small room with these grotesque glasses trying to get by one another without causing that loud CHINK and having to say "Oh cheers, I like your work." Some old and very fine writers get cornered by their large glasses somewhere at the back of the room and there is no way of getting them out without breaking them. They stare out at us like bloated pressure fish, totally enraged, wanting terribly to snap at the younger writers. I am just a drunk punk who somehow got into this pitiful ballroom. I am the kid— a baby under glass, teetering under my big drink as though it were an idol brought in from India— definitely the most important thing in the room. I came by cab for this free drink and the next— as many gigantic glasses as there are, tilting them back into my tiny throat until my head is swimming. Just as the literary firemen come in with hammers to free the old writers at the back of the room I make a last trip to the bartender. He speaks in a strange accent, deep underwater tones I can hardly understand. "In Argentina," he says pouring me another tall one, "In Argentina they torture their writers. In Canada they throw literary parties."

The Escaped Cock

For a long time the escaped cock worked in a welfare office gathering contempt for humanity. Dressed in a hat it learned to speak in a deep voice, practising by saying "No, no, no, no, no, no, NO!" over and over again. At night the cock could go home and deflate. It would lie around limp on its bed, curled up like a huge worm dreaming of power and smelling of aqua velva. The cock would not accept that it had no bones— that it was just blind flesh. Desperately the cock began to don new disguises and wander. The cock in Washington. The cock hanging around outside gun stores. The cock eating human food— meat, meat, meat. For a while the cock wore a dress and pretended to be a woman, but the cock wanted to know about murder so it joined the army. There it volunteered for firing squads whenever it could and so came to shoot human being after human being until it no longer felt anything about them— shooting them through the heart, shooting them in the mind, shooting and shooting and shooting. As time went by the cock began to rise through the ranks from soldier to sergeant to major. A general! Always a loner. Four stars— a sham, an inhuman thing, an alien presence in the army. But now the cock could get close to the bombs, the great fertile bombs, bombs like eggs in underground ranks. The cock had the power. It could rub its face on the bombs, mad about having no bones, a little crazy, bursting at odd times into tears, but a good soldier. Not so good on TV though. The face twitched. What if they uncovered the awful truth? This was no human being. This was an awful escaped cock. This was the big, violent Dick, the maniac genital. This was the terrifying schizophrenic cock— the killer cock of the world. There was a tense moment when the cock was asked its first question— "Now tell us General LeCoq, to your knowledge was the army in any way involved in this?" The cock took a hanky and wiped some sweat from its glans. Then it spoke in its deepest voice. "No, no, no, no, no, no, NO!" answered the cock.

Precautionary Chandeliers

For some, luck has the thickest thread and it hangs them over the world like little Christs for a while. The bullets go bouncing in the grand ricochet— the pin-ball of america all lit up in neon and you never know when that thread will fray in a wedding vow, snap in a brake cable or simply come undone in some madman's mind. For some, fate's thread is just the line a big fish snaps— or just the wire a puppet dangles from, for yes, all are swung on ropes round and round in a huge tangle like intersecting yo-yos. For others, no matter how consistently they turn, seemingly in balance, slowly winding up the long thread of their days into marriages and coffins, no matter how consistently they spin round their deeds, there will always be a chance of fate's big career knocking them off course, over-turning families, sending children scurrying out in huge automobiles, launching astonished girls in cradles over rooftops, ejecting wives and husbands from living rooms with dogs in the big doppleganger. And so it is that the big science of prediction puffed up in computery and fed by stealth, employed at any cost as telescope to the well-established neighbourhoods. I warn you though, no matter how many times you sit in that armchair, no matter how many times you pace that circle, inserting the protection like clock-work, establishing the blood in concentric circles on the moon, no matter with what consistency you pace out the dull legions of your one day there is always that small chance, some small snapping of something somewhere will send a grotesque item hurtling through your picture window— a gigantic greek talisman perhaps, a white alarming dog or a yo-yo of bones snapped by some punky god. There will be a ricochet at light-speed shattering the glass to crystal and great fish of flame leaping up. That is when, if you have been careful, we may see you swinging above them, safe in your precautionary chandeliers.

The Uncatchable Man

There was once an uncatchable man and nothing could catch this man, not traps, not houses, not colds, not people with nets, nothing could catch him because he was free and easy and he couldn't be nailed down. He just travelled around in search of a special jewel he was after and would slip out of any sticky situation with a high squeal and some very fine rolling. Eventually the uncatchable man found his way to a certain pollen patch, and, being very white he decided to roll there taking on for a while the fabulous rainbow hues of nature. While he was rolling there, rolling and laughing about how easily he had always evaded capture, the resident butterfly came by and asked him, "How are you liking the trap?" "What do you mean the trap?" he asked. "The trap you're in," the butterfly replied. "You are caught in a butterfly trap." "Ah-ha-ha!" the man laughed, for he knew the butterfly was wrong and that nothing could catch him. "Well why don't you leave then?" the butterfly asked. "I could leave if I wanted to," the man yelled, continuing to roll— rolling, if anything, more joyfully and laughing louder and louder as he moved deeper and deeper into the pollen trap. Rolling and laughing and thinking about how much capture he had evaded and chortling with shrill glee. "Bet you can't get away now," the butterfly screamed above him. "Bet you like the trap now." "O how I love the trap," the man yelled. "I love the trap— so much fun to get away from. So much fun to roll like this, right up to the stickiest flowers themselves and then run away." Saying this the man pointed to the bent-down lips of a huge pollen-swollen flower which was at the very heart of the trap. "Aaaaah what a sweet flower!" he said in a high hysterical voice, observing with great appetite the sticky climb of pollen higher up the blue and red and purple petals. Suddenly he felt a great urge to stick his face right up one of the large floral bells. "Watch this," he said to the butterfly, and getting down on his multi-coloured knees and folding back his pollen-smeared wings he ducked his head down under right up into the open mouth of it. "O sweet, sweet sticky colours!" the man giggled from within, letting the multi-coloured syrups ooze down onto his shoulders and draw him in. "O sweet and tasty flower!" he bellowed. And then of course, just as it looked like he had been captured he popped out with a shriek of triumph, jumping up and down mockingly in front of the butterfly. "Well, bye-bye butterfly," he said, turning his back on her as he ran across the pollen patch and out into the world. Bitterly the butterfly watched the uncatchable man go running and then she returned weeping to her nest at the top of the flowers. Some day her tender blossoms would be restored. Some day she would catch a mate. Sadly, sadly as the moonlight fell and the great whoops and shrieks of laughter of the uncatchable man faded into the starlight and dew the tears of the butterfly dripped down the stalks of her flowers and formed for an instant a jewel— that very jewel which the uncatchable man was, even now, frantically searching for.

Moth

Now you have caught in the web of your thighs, beautiful in the dew, the dark fly of my body, I will spread my wings wide and we will forever be joined here by whirlwinds and earthquakes. My love will spread out in the darkness anointing all parts of your body with a deep indelible oil, coming in on your coastlines— a dark ring and the wriggling of whales, coming in like morning, babe, spreading the holy rush of my light like a bright drug to addicted eyes. I think I will slide over the roofs of houses, down eaves and into streams. I'll be in the water that you worship with or burning on you— going up like straw, bright as a heap of roses and magnesium. Falling on you like a hawk, like stardust, like a large snowflake, instantly melting, my uniqueness gone, my white shape gone as I am joined by you in the Humanity of water.

My Body

Fallen from the heights onto your body
my body broken on your body
trashed on your body
My body is a wave that has been dashed against your body
It is the arrival like bells of a grape
upon your body, a well of brass, a love-gong
that I with full flesh set ringing
My body is a wing of lead falling
through the rainbow
The widespread wing of lead that lands
in the dark and burning oil of your body
in the smoke and the heat of your body
A beautiful moth caught in the burning pigments
of your body
its white wings fluttering in the purple and fire
as it burns
My body is an orange moon in green water
sinking in some foreign sea
It is the drop of rain, the red leaves drifting
the snows, the grasses, the torrents
My body is the dew, beautiful on blades of longing
running into you from meadows
from mists and petals
a billion bright drops in a river in the sun
It is your body looking back—
A bird sipping at its own reflection
My body on yours is a lion
in the Africas
wild with the scent of wind tawny and free,
perched on its high ledge
ready to fall
onto the back
of the earth

Poem for a Fisherwoman 1983

On a long holy strand of my finest spit I am fastening a hook to the heavens— a silver hook and a wish made of will. You, my love, are the bait— you and the boy and the family. If they will swallow that then we just might catch an angel. We just might fly. Otherwise we will climb, fixed to one another by faith and suspicion— man, woman and child high in the sun— that thin strand stretching beneath us threatening to break. I am drawing in a golden globe of undying fish, flipping even now in my palm, holy and alive in my lips. Ah sweet love, on a thin green strand of phlegm I am drawing a hospital in— a holy hospital of brutalized angels. Angels who won't do. Big church angels and some commercial angels too. I have caught a bottle of holy glue, the same holy glue that god uses, fastening himself to the religions. Fast holy glue that sets in a second and I am spreading it on the earth for you hoping for just a touch of paradise, some little soul-bit of me in you to settle down. We will touch, we two. We will embrace and afterwards because of it, no matter how thin, our bodies and our souls will always be joined by a little strand. So, babe, wind me in. Take me down off the rooftops. Pull me out of the deep rapids, the highest part of the sky where the cold wind goes by. Draw me in from streets miles away by magic. And never cut this strand. Never even try for there is not one blade, not one twilight, not one sharp mouth deep enough for that. You will always be joined to me now, slender fisherwoman. Just you and Saturn on a string. You and the world hanging from a thread with your heart and your lust and your blood. So draw down heaven love. Tug that silver string and drag this kite out of the whirlwind. Come, into this gamble, this boat pulled into the unknown— this journey in the wild current.

Tales of a Domestic Heart

I turn off the switch to your heart. Your heart goes out, with no glowing. Your heart, your heart. I have a special blinder, a piece of fine lead for your heart. I have a parasol and sunglasses for your heart. A special myopia developed over years of staring— years of squinting into mirrors searching for beauty. Now I can't see your heart. O blow it up, my loved one— swell it up and over til it's everywhere.

Your heart is squeezed into the corner. It is under the bed. Always scurrying from vision. Your fugitive heart. Silent, obvious. Your huge heart red and sore. Your angry heart sick of being silent and invisible. Your heart needs a shake-up. If you re-do your heart, then, when it is huge and stuck on a chair weeping, perhaps I will see it. Take off the blinders to your heart. Get your heart out of its scared shell. I want to see your heart. Please send me your heart. Let's strip your heart.

When she is angry she throws her heart in the bath. Huge and wooden it just sits there floating, cracking and splintering. I open the door and say, "Are you all right?" I go over and kiss her heart, burning my lips, forgetting the great heat of her heart. The heart just floats in the bath. I can hear it hissing. Push the heart under— it comes to the surface. I say sorry to her heart. Next thing she puts her heart up on a pole in the living room. She walks around looking sullen, doing the dishes. "What's wrong?" I ask her. "Nothing," she answers, but the heart swells and lets out a huge *crack* on top of the pole. I go quietly and take the heart down from off the pole, open the windows, get sunshine on her heart. Still she is in the kitchen doing the dishes. Becoming cruel, I put it down with the pots and pans and leave her in there furiously weeping and scrubbing, the heart still beating in the leftover soup.

Finally I take her to bed and curl round it. I curl round it like a foetus. I curl round it til it as big as a boulder and I am like a tiny leech, a tiny worm in her heart. I curl round it under the covers until she comes to bed for it. She slips in beside me deathly cold, her feet like stones and then in the darkness I open her ribs and slip it in. It will only work for a while— enough for a little peace to make her warm. I put her heart back in behind her breast and I rub her til it is beating madly. I rub her til the heart is all stoked up and then when it goes off, I go to sleep.

In the morning her heart is breaking through again. She takes it off with her to work. She keeps it in a purse, in a bell and some cups. In the morning her heart is small and efficient. It is rolled up in leaves and left for the children, left for the winds and workers til she returns. Her heart. Her beautiful heart.

Poem for a Tall Woman

If you have ever seen the green in water that is forever flowing out to mystery and adventure then you know something of the colour of her eyes. I would not talk so foolishly but there is a space in me that she steps into— a tall shadow, an absence that howls like a grave or a dead wind when she is not there. I am a fool for her, letting all of me be a mile long night breeze if she is but a straw held up— a single golden hair that I might rush over forever. I love Marsha Kirzner like the taste of my own spit, like my own blood in my veins, ready to melt in her heat like snow carried south and dropped in Pacific surges, my mouth dissolved in tropical mangoes and sweet papaya. She is another tall self I keep inside and lean on like a prop— a magic self that sets me whirling and dispersing— an anchoring self like a two-tone idol thin and heavy in the bed, me fastened to it like a small burnt lizard. Let me just hold this mantis woman in my arms, this tall beautiful fire with green eyes. Let me just lick the length of this green blade, this lightning filament of her love and I will sizzle, yes I will sizzle with it, a long green furrow in my spirit where a jade lake reaches for the peaks. Her hand is like a leaf that can calm the passage of a storm and yet it is a leaf that sings in its work like a reed made of Human flesh, a musical flesh of gasps and sighs— a high sweet strand of water that is like a violin string. Aaaah draw the bow down again my loved one across the heart, across the soul, draw the bow down again and play forever the long sweet notes of our love.

Now There Is Rain

Where your eyes were now there is rain
and where your lips were now there is anguish
O where the touching was
now, Rafiki, now there is pain
your absence so awesome to us
we ache outside it
like children in a winter

O what a long cold wind your death sends
whistling through us
What a galaxy of tears— tears that shine
with your grace remembered.

Where your brown skin was
now the leaves drift past
It is one of those days
always one of those days when pain gnaws in the air
pain in the brittle grass
and the distant cruel sun

Aaaaaah Rafiki my sweet babe
no more can I cup my hands
into the water of your life and see myself
gleeful in your love
no more the rain of your life upon my life
so bright, so bright in the days
You are gone in the river of light, my child
over smooth lands to the sea you go
dissolved in the sun at the edge of the world

Your soul in its star— distant and beautiful
cut from us in time
in your little boat

Wait for us my child
beyond the reefs of eternity.

for Rafiki Cruise
April 1, 1978 — October 28, 1981

The Man with the Nitroglycerine Tears

The man with the nitroglycerine tears, his sorrow terribly intact, stared from a window and waited for rain. It was amazing how much pain he kept bottled up in blue and white eyes— thick, compressed pain like sap colouring his features in deep rings of rage, spreading out like poison to the rim of his fingertips. If the trees were this full of pain they would twist in agony, making hideous shapes over graveyards, screaming with the wind, black howls from Hell on Earth. Aaaah the pain that would not leak out of his eyes. How this pain thickened in his throat, the hands grasping like roots in his sleep, mad, in a frenzy to be caught up in something. Perhaps he would fly and weep in an airplane, the bright explosions of his tears like bombs in the night below him. Weep over the barracks, weep over the parliaments. Weep, sobbing with grief over churches and educational institutes. For so long he had hidden those nitroglycerine tears in the pockets of his eyes and he was dreaming through them, fantastic griefs. He thought of his mother, of children. He thought of love he could not be reached by and imagined midnight arms factories lighting up the dark skies with his aerial grief. One morning he woke up and as though coming through the high dome of a cathedral the sunlight streamed in through a large tear which had somehow escaped during the night and now lay quivering, explosively on his cheek. For hours he lay there tilting his head back without blinking, letting gravity slowly draw the tear back into his eye, hardly daring to breathe lest he explode.

One day in the street like a great wave it finally overcame him. He sobbed, bent over and watched as the first two great luminous teardrops hurtled down to the pavement. As he wept louder and louder the man was blown apart, sizzled, ruptured, burnt by grief saying "Aaaaah children, children, children. My babes, my babes."

Only a few pieces of the man with the nitroglycerine tears were found— an eyelid in Kenora, an arm in Minsk, a lot of blood in Lake Erie and in various parts of Northern Ontario small red pieces of his heart. These were gathered up and put to rest beneath a stone which read: HERE LIES THE MAN WITH THE NITROGLYCERINE TEARS. Of all things in life, he loved rain best.

Sometimes There Is a Way

I touch my soul to yours at the mouth and two needles knock in our hearts. Self-absorbing colours mix in heat maps— purple and red turning gold, all the colours of creation flashing through us in neon pulses as we writhe. Aaaah give me the touch of my lover's hand upon my neck like a brush in paint. Give these colours in my head the touch of spirit her eyes will need. Sometimes there is a way. Get your love to lay you down ten miles long and be a lake in the sunset— a long thin finger lake, a lake that darkens with pain and mystery in the evening, rising up and menacing the cliffs of love. Let your love then lay upon the stillness at the centre of you a hand that spreads it, calming you out to a lapping and shimmering in a moonlight that is green. O sometimes there is a way out of human agony my love. Sometimes we can move with kisses dark rivers of pain in the throat. There are regions of sunrise in my being which can break their boundaries and spread if you but touch the key. O I am here to announce that there definitely is a way, and our bodies, our gestures are maps to it that we must follow like blind ones touching each curve of braille in ecstasy as we wander along the blonde and tawny roads.

Eggshell Children

Eggshell children are our most fragile and precious resource. They can grow into great diviners, trekkers to water, discoverers of fabulous new lyrical machines. If they can grow into human reeds there will be a white kind of moonlit magic again. But with even the most tolerant of parents an eggshell child is in constant danger. You see, eggshell children want to last forever. They want to be free and always have their own way. They scream and cry at amazing volumes and cannot be dissuaded from expressing rage, terror and despair, and though they also excel at having fun, at bringing delight, there are times when their parents feel like handling them roughly. Usually much violence has been done to the parents in their own childhoods but they are big, meaty, solid people, not delicate instruments of music like the eggshell child. One fist could cave an eggshell child in completely and it would lie dying, broken into fine blue shards. This has led to a proliferation of forums on the care of eggshell children. Here are some of the basic rules:

When they are born do not hold them upside down by the feet and smack their bottoms to wake them up as this will ruin their little eggshell arses. Do not deliberately put them in rocking cradles on window sills in the breeze. Watch your subconscious urges with them, don't suddenly forget and go to clap them on the back. Don't throw them a rock, a hard ball, a spoon. Don't grab their hands when they try to run away from you. Don't pull their teeth out with strings and doorknobs and finally do not slap eggshell children's faces in anger as this can not only completely ruin their cheeks but also crush leagues and leagues of delicate diamonds in their eyes.

The School behind the School

Certain people feel that there is much to be gained in life from an ability to sit together in neat little rows of about ten— five rows side by side. To this end they have built large walled buildings and therein train their children from an early age to resist all the temptations there are to rise up and go outside and play. Initially there is an adjustment period during which they do not aggravate the young ones unduly, but very soon they begin to test the children's willpower with shrill chalk screams, cackling old ladies and nasty men in square hats. If they can sit in these neat rows and learn to memorize facts for a period averaging 17 years, then upon passing a certain prescribed examination they are deemed to be graduates of the school itself and thereafter fit to be playground instructors, ministers of recreation or revolutionaries. The entire education is not complete however unless they have passed the awful truth test. At some point during their endurance of the long training process, somewhere among history lessons, seminars on mathematics and spelling bees, somewhere in the midst of all this the awful truth becomes visible to them for one searing second. If the child can maintain his or her composure when this happens and not rush from the room holding his or her head with both hands and screaming, the child will have passed the most important test there is in education and shall then be considered a graduate of the school behind the school.

Poète

Somehow the education hasn't ruined her mind. Every night she comes alone to a place no leading hand took her to. Alone she lies down in it. One night a river bed, another night a well and every night in her own way beneath a single star she focuses on the lover, the star, the well, whoever it may be. Visionary she has his dream-eyes, his green country by heart. She has his hand and his heart. Somewhere near the sea shore she loses all shape, becomes the reed, the weed, whatever drifts along. Somewhere in the ecstasy of finally losing herself, the poem comes and as though all the fish at once leapt up onto banks and started wriggling there in an important ecstatic fury she attacks the typewriter so that from that clacking and clicking, before she goes on finally to the ocean, something of the current, the weed, the gull is born and remains.

Adventures of My Hand

As far away as my pocket, as close as your breast, my hand cannot get to the banquet on time. It is coming in from a far-off place, on a rocket, on a train. My hand the worker— a gigantic fist kept in a stall, pounding in fury. My hand in a suit pretending to be a man on some luxury liner crossing its legs. My hand is a great poet always writing. I remember it coming back from the factory crushed in a machine when I was sixteen— a fat mottled rainbow, huge as the hand of a god— a great fist in bed. I remember it slipping like silver into those rollers coming out crushed flat— a white web of bones til the blood held back rushed in to fill it, to rejoice in its return, shocked, running over the broken vein mouths, bleeding ever and ever inward— a huge gush down from the wrist that would blacken and rot. My hand screaming. My hand in bandages— those fat purple fingertips, that burnt palm, that swollen wrist— all of me threatening to bulge out into this multi-coloured bruise. My hand Joseph. My hand Jacob and Christ and Neruda. My hand the rebel, the fist, tied down by a million machines but still rising in the air, still smashing down on the earth, snapping the threads, grasping and clawing its way to freedom. My hand is hunted now. It wanders over the world in search of its own kind. It goes from door to door trying to be joined up to something, knowing it is just a small piece of the puzzle.

The Man Who Broke Out of the Letter X

Once while the soldiers were asleep a man broke out of the letter X. He burst through its centre and emerged into the world in a loincloth and began to run. He was past the soldiers before they could see him and when they did see him they just stood there rubbing their eyes and wondering if he was real. The man ran through the winding streets of the city faster and faster in apparent terror and many people saw him as he darted here and there along the cobblestones. As the day progressed and the streets contained more and more people, the man who had broken out of the letter X would suddenly find himself face to face with a pedestrian. When this happened his terror would redouble and he would dart off quicker and quicker, shrieking as he continued his flight. Soon the news spread that a man had broken out of the letter X and there began to be a great deal of apprehension about him. Where had he come from? What did he want? Why did he flee from them as though they were monsters?

The governor approved the order and helicopters were sent to follow the man who was running. Faster and faster he ran, his lungs burning up and coughing as he scrambled and fled across the plains and plazas of that immense city. Cars screeched to a halt, crowds gasped as he ran by. As the police began to close in on him, the man was like a tiger in the jungle, scrambling up walls, leaping up stairs, jumping over the canyons between small buildings. They caught him at last in a net. A very beautiful man— a man as beautiful as they had ever seen. But when the flashbulbs went off and he looked into the faces of his captors, he let out shrieks of horror which were like nothing they had ever heard expressed before. As he screamed, the man went into a spasm, his back arched under him, his jaw clicked open, his eyes bulged, and all of him trembled like a leaf of death. And so he died, this man who had broken out of the letter X. And why he came here and what he was running from no one ever knew, but from then on the soldiers guarded the letter X with greater vigilance, so that if anyone else broke out they could send him back inside for his own good.

The Birth of a Tree

Recently a woman gave birth to a tree. Imagine the amazement on the faces of the delivering doctor and nurses when the first of the blue branches began to peek out. Each time the mother moaned and screamed more and more of the undeveloped twigs, stunted branches and tiny little leaves came curling out. When with a great push the trunk had finally been passed and the wideness of the base emerged, the roots followed with very little effort and the delivering team stared amazed and frightened at what had come into the world.

Immediately upon being delivered, the small purpling tree began to writhe around, shuddering and shaking. The tiny roots and branches convulsed, clenching in and out like multiple fists and then the tree let out a cry. A cold lizard-like scream of anguish which seemed to them as loud as the shriek of a jet plane. A deep jungle kind of screaming though, an ancient anguished swamp-infected note that shook every one of them with the resonance of its agony. The doctors and nurses stood helplessly by while the tree screamed louder and louder, the blue limbs bucking in the sheets, the leaves shuddering like hearts, like broken mirrors, quivering and shining in the bright, bright hospital light.

They were frightened by the hideousness of the baby tree— almost incapacitated in their task, but they were professionals and somehow managed to regain calm enough to look to the needs of the mother.

When it became apparent that by some miracle, she had not suffered undue internal damage from the birth of the tree but seemed neither more nor less torn up than from the birth of a normal child, she began to cry out "Please, please, help my baby, my baby," for the tiny bruised-looking tree was starting to split itself open with the exertion of its weeping, coming undone outwardly with a fleshier and fleshier appearance, howling in horror and agony. Thankfully, one of the attending nurses then had a great flash of insight. She wheeled the tree over to the mother so that she could reach out her hand and touch it for the first time. There was a clemency, a cold distilled feeling in the air, a sound— almost a hiss, and then abruptly, reassured, the frightened baby tree became quiet.

The Mad Hand

Once there was a floating walking hand which went round and round the world darting and crawling hoping to evade detection, sometimes scaring drunks and small children. A wild leaping scampering hand not wishing to be part of a circus but utterly mad, knowing only old routines and concentric habits like circles at the bone— to dance, to tap, and insanely to shake hands. That's why this hand took to creeping into embassies and literary parties, so that it could crawl up table legs, wait for the right moment and then dive into a handshake, usurping the place of the intended other hand with a shrill kind of scream. This is the hand that madly signed papers over and over again, pouring wine glasses back into nothingness, tilting back beers, making its stump shriek like a whistle.

For a while the hand hung out with spiders thinking it might be one of them, not knowing that it was really an insane disconnected hand— a writher, a dancer, it dreamed of running over buttons like a minefield, setting off sequences of roses in some drunkard's head, detonating poems like Q-blasts. "ARRRRG! Take me to the abodes of people! Get me into a glove! I will buck and jolt. I will seize up and spit blood if I do not get involved in a caress."

One thing the hand liked to do was grope and poke at parties— touch people in places no living human being could get at— give a poke in the dark and then roll across the floor like a combat-trained creature, chuckling with sheer unbearable squeals as the puzzled party-goer nervously eyed whoever was behind him.

Sometimes the hand liked nothing better than to ride the still surface of a stream like a water spider— to just hang there above its own reflection, each finger as it touched the mirror leaving a poem to the sky, an ode to the sun, a divine literature.

Also it is true that the hand would sometimes go into a factory, start up the assembly belts and madly assemble amazing gadgets, strange amalgams and marvellous gimmicks, all the while whistling with its strange humour until it fell down exhausted.

Of all things, the hand most enjoyed slapping the faces of dictators when they made big speeches on television. This made the hand well-known to all dictators, but due to the fact that these programs are pre-taped, the mad escaping hand never had the pleasure of having its handiwork seen by the people. So if you ever see a political speech and after the commercial the great leader comes back on looking a little stunned, a widening red imprint spreading out on his cheeks, look at that shape, that map, that message in the right light and you will see it for what it really is— the mark of a mad hand.

My Huge Voice

I was born with a huge voice and I lay there with a huge voice in a new world my voice too big for me. When I screamed I shook birds from the roof. My father called me big mouth and went to sea. My father came back and beat my voice and my voice got harder and harder. My mother grew my huge voice in a pot. She put its feet in the cradle and gave it a story at bedtime. As the body grew the voice grew larger and larger, stronger and stronger. Soon I was dragging this huge voice through the public school system, sometimes hardly able to fit through doorways my voice was so huge and so stuck in my throat, and though I rarely sang, though I only whistled, though I talked at normal volume my voice was huge and I knew it. Finally at the age of twenty I began to let my voice go. My voice that was gigantic. Which if I screamed could shake temples, topple towers and blast leaves from entire trees. Slowly I let my voice unwind. I let it shake and shatter as it welled up, lying back blasted open almost broken by the voice blaring up out of me. It is hard to be a body for a voice like this— a huge voice that wants to be heard everywhere. Sometimes I try to keep quiet and end up shouting. Sometimes I lie down. I try to go to sleep all swollen up with this voice and it is too late to sing, too dark to speak so I must lie there til the morning utterly silent, my body, an elastic to the sun, a small halter the voice is breaking through, my mind just a trembling seed for the wonder of this voice.

Fear of Hands I

My father could bear no sign of what he called "arrogance" in me. Frequently and without warning he would slap me or punch me, shouting "Get that bloody arrogant look off your face." Somewhere along the line I was eroded. I became for a time a grinning shit-eater. Polite and, when alone with myself, dangerous.

I remember once, after having been wrongfully assaulted and sent to my bedroom, I was biting my lips, gnashing at the bedroom sheets in my rage, tearing at my own body in my fury, when suddenly the scream burst out of me. "YOU PRICK!" And what a huge, bloody, raw-throated holler it was. Not only did it seem to shake my own being, but it must have also shaken the very foundations of our house. In the split second before I heard my father's ferocious "WHAT!" I lay there with a surprised grin on my face, loving myself supremely.

Then the stampede started. My father burst into the room, his eyes nearly popping out with rage as he began to punch and wallop me in a frenzy. I felt caught in the centre of a storm. This mad berserker might kill me. After a time it stopped and all was silence. He went off, that man who is so much like me. He went off still full of rage and probably terror at what he might have done. He went off to his private place, raging and shaking and thinking who knows what tormented thoughts and left me there in the silence of myself.

My own rage was expressed. I had mollified myself with that scream. I could still believe in my own soul. What he felt he would have to tell you himself. I am no reader of closed books.

Now like a dagger my mind lunges into another memory and quivers there before me in dizzying reverberation. It is like a strobe light flash into a dark cubed room. My brother, my sister and I are there. We are small and helpless. I am grinning my sick lopsided grin. The vision that is flashed in on me, freeing us from the timeless stasis of Forget is my father with the kitchen knife. He is standing with his belly thrust forward sweating and shining in the twilight like some kind of obscene Buddha. Poised above his belly gripped tight and trembling in his two hands is the knife. He is shaking with strange unknowable passion and there is in his eyes a look of desperation and— and how shall I say it? *Longing?* There is a look in his eyes that still stares up from the bottom of my soul in dreams and yes, I will call it longing. I will call it fear and fury and desperate deprivation. He is showing us this look that is burning into us and branding us and shouting as the knife quivers in his grip— "DO YOU WANT ME TO? DO YOU WANT ME TO?" And his voice— it is as though twisted from an old rag. A worn imploring statue might grind out such a voice. An aging grey oak might talk in such a voice.

"DO YOU WANT ME TO? DO YOU WANT ME TO?" And we are saying nothing. Not daring to look at one another. Not daring because I am thinking to myself, "Well gee, dad, you know, it's up to you." And if I look at my brother I might giggle.

"Ted!" my mother screams. "TED!" and black opiate blood streams down over the window, the house falls, time slants sideways and I am there and I am here and I am there and I am here.

Fear of Hands II

There was a corner in the countertop that led to the stove
and my father had wedged my mother into it and with the full

pressure of his hand round her throat was bending her over
backwards as he strangled her. Even as I cringed there

against the wall with my brother and my despised
    smaller sister,
even in my extreme terror I thought that it was just like them

to be doing something so like out of a movie. Terror.
Increasing terror as it continued— this pressure
    round her neck,

this pulse of white polar terror in my hands, then self disgust,
terror, terror, until, aaaaah relief blue in the face,

my dear little sister, my little buster brown bruiser ran forth,
somehow out of the trance, kicked him and in her little voice

shouted "STOP IT! STOP IT!" and he did.

My Father's Hands

My father had so many hands. He had almost three. My father had almost three hands but not enough to touch me once gently. O my father had so many eyes. He had so many blue eyes. He had almost three. But not enough to see me once perfectly. O my father had but one mouth and one heart to lift those bales and bales at the factory. O my poor father of fists and fists and fists beating on the wall, beating at his brow, beating at his children. My poor factory father, lined and fat-bellied now, tranquillized and happier, made smaller by so many sons. The winds gave him only one heart and they said, "Here, spin it, make it the hole in rock we whistle shrill through. Grit your teeth and count your children." He wonders what to do with hands now. Where to put them. These tender lined things that ache for sons. O my father we are here, the prints of wanting emblazoned on us like radioactive brands. O my father had so many hands and he waves them now ashamed a little. Looking puzzled as we leave at the movement from his wrist as if he wondered, "What are they when they are not fists?"

In Stupid School

In stupid school they hated our guts and taught us the stupidest things they could think of. Geography had France located in Namibia and the Persian Gulf a subject of the Mississippi. It was good to learn false geography they told us so that later when we were travelling we would have the advantage of not knowing what country we were really in. This would make us much more employable. Falseness and confusion were my two great subjects— to make up the past each time anew. They spliced together old clips, dull montages, the worst in humour, failed jokes, commentaries for morons and told us that this was history. I can't tell you the tirades of ridicule they put us through. The taunts and insinuations that were hurled at us in the name of basic grammar. "You are scum. You were scum. You will be scum." It was insulting. For a religious exercise each day we were forced to bow and salaam to our desks, the boards, the teachers' hems, all the while chanting absurd prayers such as "Please let us go on being excrement. Please let us continue to be useless shit." All to convince us that the world was stupid. That it was run by the stupid. That it was owned by the stupid and you would be best to make yourself as stupid as possible in order to be fully employable when you were older. The problem was our innate intelligence. Some of us couldn't believe the facts put out by such schools. We tried and tried but we failed in our education. We could not get certificates which assured us we were stupid and so now no one will hire us. What a fate! While our more stupid friends secure jobs in offices and factories we must stand idly by, too smart to do anything but collect the dole, the dole, the dole.

I Knew I Could Sing (Industrial Accident No. 1)

I knew I could sing
when my hand got sucked into the rollers at the factory
cause I hit a high note then that they said
was heard over the sound of the machines
all the way up to the front office

Even as the rollers whirred and burned
and gnawed at my flesh
my mind in its detached way
was listening to that note
marvelling at its purity

I was deep in shock
by the time the men ran over
and finally turned the machine off
The great cylinder ground to a stop
and just weighed down there—
a painful rim
like a whole world
squashing my hand

When they finally unscrewed the housing
(there was no safety release at all)
it took three men to lift up
the great fallen log of the roller
and then as the blood rushed back in
to the white branch of my hand
I knew I could sing
I knew I could sing

Why I Crushed My Hand

I crushed it for my girlfriend
I crushed it for my dad
I crushed it for my mom and my squashed history
in the head
I crushed it for factory safety—
a young martyr at sixteen
I crushed my hand because I wanted to see what it was like
for the school system and workmen's compensation
just to have a story
because there was a piece of paper caught in the roller
and I wanted to get it out
so I grabbed at it and got sucked in
feeling a great tug on the flesh
all the way up my arm
I crushed my hand for world peace because I wanted to stop
the fighting in viet nam
no— I wanted to get out of my homework
I wanted people to stop hitting me
and I wanted a kiss from those
Indian lips of hers
those dark kisses
of Shamim*

I crushed my hand because I hated working in the factory
I wanted to be out in the sun and I wasn't having this
60 dollars a week
40 dollars a week is what I got on compensation
and this skin graft on my hand
where the flesh was burned off in an oval egg shape

I crushed my hand because I wanted to get the paper out of the rollers

because I had heard the story over the supper table
a million times before
because I wanted to know the careless violence of machines—
metal without pity, just power surging—
to sing, to do a great circus act, a man with a hand like a white leaf
WHOOP, a man with a hand like steak
a purple football, a man with a hand like a great yellowing yam
big as hell in the bed, in the cast
I crushed my hand to give starving doctors work
to keep the hospital going
because I wanted to see what plastic surgery was like
I was young and I wanted to meet a physiotherapist
I had never had manual whirlpool baths before
and my guts, my guts were ready because it was the damn hand
that picked up the phone, that got the news, that got the refusal
the rejection, blackened by plastic over the wires—
a baleful voice saying no saying no

because it had dared wave goodbye
because it had been in the service of the empire and was tainted
and needed to be punished
now I wouldn't have to do my share of the housework
I could just walk around with that large bandage,
the hand held high, in traction
as though in greeting and look like a holy man or a fool
I crushed my hand to find the hidden map in the flesh
that would lead me to poetry, to you and to the page
I crushed it to get out of there and get my ticket stamped
and get on with it.

*my first girlfriend (a native of South Africa) who had recently rejected me.

Industrial Accident No. 2

One minute the fingers were quite straight
and beautiful
I was pushing a plank lengthwise
into a table saw and I said to myself—
"Be careful now— your hand is getting close to the blade
and you've already had one accident."
Then the buzz saw bit into me
with a singing twang
splattering blood over three walls
in a wide halo of drops

My hand seemed to be ringing
like a bell as
I held it up in horror—
all the fingers exploded outward
like red flowers at the tips
My other hand grasped
tourniquet-tight about the wrist.
"Take me to the hospital" I screamed
jumping up and down

Now one finger is permanently bent and stiff
On cold days I don't dare type with it
and it is useless for picking up dimes
Nor is it good for pointing out directions or fault
knowing as I do
that finger is always somewhat
pointing back at me

Little Hurts

Little hurts gather in his brow, waiting to go puff, waiting to go pop in a face of rage. Little hurts burrowing down to make room. Compressed voices, things he should have said. Aaaaah little hurts like grain inside, like fields of broken barley, like dots pushed out. Little hurts on the bead a string of sweat provides. Little hurts on the abacus his fingers move along in dream-time. He is a water that life has plunged to the bottom of, his hand a catacomb of pain, his body honey-combed with grief with little hurts like pellets, like moles, like darker eyes within his eyes.

The Violent Man's Hand

The violent man's hand fell into the dust and withered to the size of a seed. Later from that spot grew the wheat that would be ground down into the earth by armies, the grains that would be burned and turned back to earth in peace.

The violent man's hand fell into the heap and from it a bird burst— a bright bursting bird, a third bird, a herd of birds so that the hand leapt and spattered as each bird burst from it. Finally it was a spent black splinter from which blue sparks leapt.

The violent man's hand sank into the earth at 2 miles per hour, heavy as lead. To come back as a bomber angel, dark lucifer jets with arms full of crosses and gelignite, dark bomber lords from hell, bleak bomber angels, that only to look into the eyes of a new born child can bring down, one by one— dark flies, dark fear-flung fists overhead, the severed hands of those who would strike us, dark wings of surrender, bleak hands of poverty thrown high.

The hand that was nailed up, crossed down, crushed at the foot. The hand that went mad and took on rage like seven gravities. That is why there are holes in Arkansas, call them comets, call them what you will. There is rage in those hands when they come down and the children run inexplicably past certain houses, terrified of a sound no one else can hear.

Poetry Is...

There are those who lay bricks
There are those who break rocks with picks
There are those who work on assembly belts
There are those who care for children
There are sex workers
and there are those who make poems

Turn on the belt and begin
the great clacking of the typewriter
smashing at the rock in the paper
thumping at the door in the paper
pushing at the bird in the paper
shaping and re-shaping the poem
holding it up to the light

There is the carpenter
and then further along down the river is the poet
filling up, systematically
the clean white rectangle
clang clang clang
his silver hammer arcs high in the sun
as he cracks through the mica surface
jang jang jang
as he shatters the diamonds there
looking for bright
truths

poetry is
manual labour

Colours of Bullshit

Out of the brain pan, then, let us spread wide the colours of bullshit like a fan, and examine them one by one. First there is red bullshit. Red is the colour of the ardent bullshit of love that is always speaking. This is the kind of bullshit that gods listen to when they need a good laugh. As a matter of fact, gods get together in groups and laugh until they are rolling when they hear the words of people in love. If they hear an exclamation such as "O my love, my love!!" it will cause them to howl. If this is followed by phrases such as "I won't ever leave you," and then a "Never?" followed by a "Never!", the gods will all shriek the word "NEVER!" together almost hurting their throats with the intensity of their mirth. Then there is blue bullshit which is the viable bullshit of the day. This is the bullshit of scientists, statisticians and psychiatrists. This kind of bullshit carries its own little tag but is nevertheless hard for the unpractised eye to detect. Listen for phrases such as "experts agree" or "statistics prove." Next in the total rainbow of bullshits comes green bullshit which is unhealthy and has lots to do with the bragging of young men in change rooms, business banter and the sickly words of deliberate seducers. Green is the colour of advertising bullshit. It is the underlying tinge of World War II bullshit. It is the green of the goitre, the fungus and the gangrene infection and is bottomed out only by that most despicable of all bullshits— white bullshit, which is of course the colour of recorded history. White bullshit is actually a very highly priced lubricant. The very one that keeps all those young bodies sliding into uniforms and all the pistons and gears of factories in motion. You have to be very careful with this kind of bullshit for it is a highly toxic, slippery and explosive substance.* When you see it recognize it. Call it by its name which is its shame. Say "Bullshit! Bullshit!"

*If you want to examine the colours of bullshit more closely yourself you can safely do this by staring at the coloured pieces of cloth which are used to attach medals to generals' chests or simply by staring intensely at the flag of almost any country.

Several Other Uses for a Halo

use it as the brim of a hat
the rim of a little wheel
put it for support in a pipe-line
up your arm and over your shoulder
reach through a halo and try
to get a hold of something in heaven
a halo is a kind of condom over your hand then
a sacrament of hygiene
a kind of navel in the sky
where you were cut
from umbilical sun-strings

dance in a hat made of the halo
shit through the halo
put your dick through the halo and pee
bounce the halo on pavement
put your halo in the hand of a friend
and entrust it there
like your own genitals
only exceedingly more tender
more sensitive
there are nerves in a halo more delicate
than diamonds
nerves that turn and receive
sending in messages and meaning
to your sensorium
put your halo back up in the sky
and look through it—
play the halo on your turntable
tie it to a dog, to a pig, to an elk, to a bison
let wild animals drag the halo off
drop the halo out of jet planes
put the halo in barbed wire
put it round a starved man
let it hover over a child
reach for your better self
through the hole in the halo
give the halo to your enemy
entrust the halo to random burials

let the halo be heaved from mound to mound in ghostly
quoits
do gymnastics on the halo, swing from the halo,
find the high arc of heaven as you let the halo go
sell the halo
melt it down and pass it round
put the halo in boxes
hammer out the haloes
long thin wire of the haloes
bury the haloes beneath the earth
mountains of haloes
mould the haloes in mammon faces
send the haloes skipping over water
gold teeth of the haloes
jewellery of the haloes

you don't need the halo any more
you are ready to let the halo go
you have to put the halo on a hook
you have to put the halo on a hook
and just walk away from it

II.
If you set up a halo in a winter sky
then, when the coldest winds howl through it
they activate old voices in misery
voices out of Hell on earth
The cries snuffed out by rifles and machetes
the cries snuffed out by grave dirt
Haloes can unleash these horrors which
are ravelled into the air
listen in the winter wind and see if you
detect the presence of fallen haloes
the pressure of punctures, bone-rimmed holes
where torment finds its stiff round mouth at last
o blow the bugles of bone
o beat the drums of bone
let the slaughtered dead arise again in song
listen
listen my christian ones
to the howling of the wind

In Drug Heaven

(God is the opiate of the masses— Karl Marx?!)
(Masses are the opiate of the Gods— Robert Priest)

In drug heaven masses are the opiate of the Gods. Gods get strung out on such masses. They write books of junky talk and need more and more masses. They die in alleys of overdoses. They rot in Olympus. Gods on smack in Valhalla. They even got some to Christ in his pain— a sponge full of junk on a stick smuggled into paradise, enough so that he couldn't hear each time someone took his name in vain. "O Christ! O Christ!" but Christ is numb on his cross. He can't care. Christ is the heroin of the masses. He aches in the addiction of the masses like an unhealing wound.

Some masses are the bennies of the Gods. Gods get fast on such masses— they sweep and sweep the floor. They look out the window a lot. They sweep the floor and walk around. They write their junky books faster and faster.

The Gods hallucinate at particularly good masses. Such masses are said to be the Acid of the Gods. O dark unconscious! Jehovah on his bad trip killing the first born. At such times Gods have to come down fast. They can't sleep when they see what they have done. They need the valium of the masses— masses and masses of valium to put them out cold. That's when they find out the terrible truth— there is no easy way out of Drug Heaven. No simple method to withdraw and forget. Just Drug Hell ever-waiting below and all the beautiful vales of earth powerless to stop them as they fall.

To Me, Eating a Piece of Meat

To me, eating a piece of meat would be like eating a blood-soaked air-conditioner filter. I can't see a steak in a frying pan without first imagining it up in the window, screening out warped genetic material, karmic gluons and irradiated pollen. Much of the meat we eat comes from animals who are kept locked up, force-fed, brutalized and degraded— chickens that have their beaks cut off so they won't peck each other to death in their agony— cattle whose legs break under the sheer weight of their own force-fed bulk. The meat we eat sinks to the bottom of us and keeps us weighed down in the pre-dawn of the Human Spirit. Always our treatment of the animals has spread to our treatment of each other. Is it any wonder then that our leaders are building an abattoir in the sky for us? What do you think— are those flags of glorious nationhood they are waving about or just pieces of meat on the end of a stick?

My Problem with the Flag

I am against the present Canadian flag. Picture it. A red maple leaf. What is a leaf? It is something that has come loose and fallen. It will become stiff and lie in heaps with other leaves. No permanence, no anchor— just one little leaf in a huge cycle. Perhaps this modesty suits us, but what about the colour— red. Too red. Redder than any real maple leaf ever gets. As a matter of fact as red as blood. Perhaps an unconscious admission of how we got the country? All our past deeds ever evident in this splayed inkblot. Then there is the rest of the design. A bar of red, a bar of white and a bar of red. Big deal— two basic colours with a kind of shotgun spatter in the middle. Why must our hopeful nation be marched beneath such an incarnadine rag? Where is imagination? Why with all our totem heritage would we hoist anything on a bare pole? Why from all our ancient forests would we seek out and wave one red and fallen leaf?

My Problem with the Canadian National Anthem

One of the worst pieces of music I have ever heard is the Canadian national anthem. It isn't the words. They seem honest enough— "O Canada our stolen native land..." but the melody, the structuring of the chords, those old tonal textures— how completely unoriginal this work is. The melody functions in absolute symmetry as though written by some kind of computing device climbing up and down scales in complete hyper-predictability. If you need anything occipuntal in music, if you require anything of cadence, lilt, metre or tone, there is none of that here. Listen again to any song you have heard and liked and something of it will be in the music to O Canada. Speed it up slow it down, the notes are there. It is a hodgepodge song, plagiarized from a thousand boring symphonies written by mediocre composers in the Old World, all of whom had been brainwashed by modern concepts and a musical education. People all around the world hear this terrible piece at hockey games and jumping matches and are sneering in their seats at the unoriginality it evinces. Two bars and in their minds they are saying "Old hack garbage!" Still they tap their feet and try to maintain their composure because they have to do business with us. What a shame that this obviously turgid composition should even be associated with this huge and varied land. All the notes are used over and over in varying fashions and arrangements but insistently with a 4/4 beat that is monotonous and military in the worst possible way.

If this weren't bad enough it is always the worst musicians who are hired to play O Canada. People who have worked hard and learned the brutish approach. Da-da-da! They have spent hours getting piles in the corner. They have bitten the insides of their cheeks off getting wild with tension and now at last they've got this trumpet part. Then due to graft it is always the shit companies that press the record. People like Quality and World who don't care dick about the product, content to put a piece of vinyl out which is almost air soluble so that by the time these vulgar recordings reach the ears of our children they are so full of hiss and static as to make the lyrics completely unintelligible. Left then only with the mundane torturous melody which is so universally despised outside of our borders is it any wonder that children are showing disrespect to some of our noblest traditions?

Silence Is Coming

Silence is coming. Silence is coming. Over the steppes of Africa, right now over wild seas, across the Pampas of Argentina. If you are in Atlanta, if you are in Berlin, Toronto, Montreal, alas, a silence is coming. I don't know what it is. It may be a wind without substance— but it is full of the cries of dead birds, full of the cry of the natives and it is moving up through the prairies of America. It is sinking in everywhere— a silence of buffalo, a silence of bison and whale. One day soon the silence will move over us and we will not at first notice it— at home in the vastness of the silence, but then it will continue for an hour and each of us, as though in a dream, beyond the reach of sound or speech, will gesture in horror at the soundless reverberation of our axes, the silent working of our machinery. The jets will go by and there will be no shrill sound. The radio will glow but there will be no static and no cry from the crushed animals who will stare up from their pain at us, the stabbed man's cry lost in the silence, the raped woman's scream absorbed in the silence and infants born into a soundless world— a world where the dog's bark goes unheeded, where the bugles blow without warning and where even the clocks lack for an hour their steady and unstoppable ticking.

Consumption

*(for John Keats)**

In Yardley Birmingham on June 30, 1984
Peter Dowdeswell ate 21 3 1/2 ounce hamburgers
(with 3 and a half inch diameter buns)
in 9 minutes 42 seconds
Karen Stevenson of Wallasey, Merseyside
on April 4, 1981 ate 2780 baked beans
one by one with a cocktail stick in 30 minutes
James Lindop in Manchester England on September 29, 1973
ate 13 raw eggs in 3.8 seconds.
"Bozo" Miller in one sitting
at Trader Vic's, San Francisco
California in 1963 ate
27 2-lb. chickens.
Jay Gwaltney consumed an 11 foot birch tree
in 89 hours
There is a man in Spain
who eats bicycles.
He files them down and swallows them with pasta.
Another man died of trying to eat a bus.**

All these people had
that famous modern disease—
Consumption—
just like John Keats.
I have it too.
I forget all about myself when I am hungry.
I'm not romantic.
I just have to stuff that next meal into my face.
I am always swallowing.
Bran muffin, *chomp chomp*, eat it
on the way home, hands shaking,
vegetable soup from a can— *glop*,
toasted English muffin with butter,
chomp chomp,
Consumption.
Coffee, dope, coffee, consume,
Consumption.
This whole society has consumption.
We are always swallowing something.

We are all suffering from that rare disease— bulimia.
We are polydipsomaniacs.
One day we will find a way to make the dirt nourishing.
Then you will see people with the soil
always in their mouths.
You will see them out in the gardens
grazing like horses. Til then
if you feel a pain, aaaaah just
drop something onto that spot.
Parachute a few chops down,
some instant potatoes,
some Maalox.
You can lose the weight later.
It's all right.
You're sick.
You have consumption, just like
John Keats.
Haven't you noticed your eating habits?
You chew on pencils.
You suck on cigars,
You smoke cigarettes.
You're always looking through your shit for signs.
Yes, you have it too.
Consume! Consumption!
Consumption!

And that child in the jungle.
She wants to eat the leaves.
She wants to gnaw on the
Stones.
Swallow the air
This is no joke to her.
She is starving.
She has our disease too.
She is dying of our disease...

Consumption.

*As a child when I first heard that Keats had died of Consumption I thought this meant
that he had eaten himself to death.
**All these statistics according to the *Guinness Book of World Records*.

152

My Infected Television

One day my television swelled up. The screen turned pink and then burst like a boil in my living room. As I watched with horror this media-esque outburst was followed by more and more colourful disgorgings. Soon this "pus" was filling up my living room and running down the window out into the street, filling up the drainage ditches with whirling pigments and condensed clotted crystals. By this time a television news crew had been called in and were now busy filming my famous occurrence. You should have seen the stunned looks on their faces when, as they interviewed each other, they noticed small digested glimmers of their own images, squashed in two, whited out and infected, gush seconds later from my infected tube. Such a gush of crushed light and poisoned vision! Greener and greener it ran— the news at the base of it all, thick and venomous, the insinuations, like subliminal toxins millowing there, taking on electrical charges from the bottom.

Only the skin of a fresh-killed lamb would stop this dangerous progress I was told so I sent for a priest. By the time he arrived the colours had stopped gushing out and had been replaced by darkness— a black thick static which seemed to be full of voices, torments from old sound-tracks, actual agonies captured on film and new things— infant squeals, dull shovel thuds of graves being dug somewhere, deeper agonies than I had ever wished to hear. The lamb was killed and skinned, the flesh held up pink and glowing over the tube and then the priest spoke some words which were in another language.

After some days when the skin was removed the glass on the front of the TV was cracked from the centre outwards in dark strands like an incendiary sun— an ash— a map like radium in the sand, a bleak staring eye. For days it healed itself until finally almost as white as an egg the eye rolled on again and let out its rainbow beam, its yellow beams of laughter, those green green golds of mirth, those wonderful blues of sky and silver.

The skin I hung, totally irradiated like a big dusty butterfly skin and have oftentimes amused myself trying to interpret the patterns which are engrained on it. They are like small encephalographs or curious runes and I am almost certain that they must mean something.

The Little Pig of Self Respect

got away from General Li Tu. It ran greased and squealing through the populace as the soldiers tried to catch it, leaving the general with a space the same shape as that pig suddenly missing from his heart. Immediately the weasels of remorse began to burrow in, looking for that absence. Hedgehogs of guilt and blood fish of anguish long held at bay sucked their way along his veins, up through the marrow, all looking for that small shivering pig-space, to live in its emptiness, to take up residence in its vacated temple— the general left writhing, sweating on the bed, beset by terrible visions, knowing there was no more pig-space inside now, just a crammed banquet hall full of ravenous mice, and gorged weasels toasting each other with his blood. No more pig-space in the soul! So that even afterwards when the little pig of self respect was dragged back to him crying and squealing he had nowhere left inside himself to put it and so had to wear it stitched down, over his shoulders like a kind of pink epaulette.

An Exhortation to Dance

You have been taken to an office stretched out in a blue suit
by red elastics and extended into a painful alphabet-like shape
that you hate
      And we are asking you to Dance
Someone has cooky-cut you just as you are.
You've always been like that— a brass monkey in the night.
You've never leapt,
You've never popped, hopped or bopped
      yet we are asking you to dance
Some have been captured by clothing and forced to mendicate
caught up and ritualized,
Some have been standing like candelabras in the rain
for ten successive generations
unable to move til they are struck by human lightning
      Well dance you strange shapes now. Dance pipes of
insignificance and elbow alphabets.
      For too long you have lain beside the ocean on the sand
      spelling out the words "I NEED" with your limbs
For too long you have lain like a brand
like a rune of misery, heavy in the earth,
the mark of a curse or a warning
You will say. I have been asleep for ten million years
I have been beaten out of metal to make this shape
My limbs are fossilized in iron habits, ancient geologies
How can such deeply held oil dance
To which I reply with drum beats
      with electric guitars in ecstasy
    with wild sedimentary singing
      that breaks up everything in the heart
because everywhere you walk there is a shadow
joined to your foot like a refugee
and you have to drag around this darkness
until you lose it in the dance
So come and undulate your essences
      part being part not being
come and beat on the beach of brass again and again

in moments of bubble time
in moments of not knowing or knowing
  o come and be one
  come and be one
    of the many

sperm sperm sperm

sperm sperm sperm
sperm sperm sperm
aaah tugging the mad kites in the testicles
sperm sperm sperm
sperm sperm sperm

an armada of sluggish stars whir their halvling fins
twirl their automatic propellers
we are sperm sperm sperm they would say
with their round white faces
just curls of information
we are genetic submarines
tender tender detonators
and if you think a man is lost, driven
imagine a sperm
only the halved makings of a man
only one instruction and motor
in row on row of coiled vegetal fire
springs of soul,
dots of lust
all just waiting for a kiss, a sight, a tremble
to be melted down at once
into white willing wax
the heat-seeking sperm
waiting to get out and expand at the stars
tracking down something to get lost in
something to be complete in

The Origin of "Woman"

Not Woe to Man
as I once thought
or even
Womb-Man
as the man-fastened
think
but
Wom*ban*
as in Terr*an*
or Afric*an*
or Canadi*an*—
e.g.
a native of the Womb
a
Womban

meaning all people
even men
are Womb-en
first

Poem for My Unborn Child

There will be a first time I will meet you
I have never seen your face
I have felt you kick, move around in your
beautiful privacy
have heard your heart like a frantic butterfly beating
beautiful and full of light
in there
the great pulse of the blood rushing through the veins
I have been frightened
startled by you
I have dreamed about you
and now I have felt your shape through your mother's belly
but I have never seen your face

yet I will love you all my life

On the Birth of My Son

I am a mad butterfly, flying in a frenzy all around him, zappy and electric, my many colours going off like city lights as I whir and flap in and in, closer to him, calming down sometimes to a condensation, a drop of water he floats in, a gentle tear, a wave that bears him dancing around the house, little king, god-prince, little guru baby, taking it all in with such calm eyes til the next time you must grimace and fart or belch or hiccup. I am a stunned follower finally, an acolyte in some religion. Aaaah what it is to be a slave to a wish, a need.

New Father

She is a warm country of milk
and I am the black side of the moon
a burned out ship floating by

She is the shoreline to safety and I am
the circus— the whirling chariots
and frightening rides

In her arms he finds the great vales of his yearning
the country he will always belong to
I am a stranded province a wandering region

of music that sings madly near him
I wish I were a star like she is to him
but, for now I must be a crazy satellite

a little too large for the house
but near her and near him. Near them.

Your Cry

Your cry is an opening in me
in my centre
in my trumpet-part
Your cry is a bell in me
ringing with an awesome
emanation
Crying for your mother
you cry for mine in me
and my father too would cry for his

Your cry reminds me that there is a cavern
in me where winds howl
a kind of Gaspé of the soul,
a need-tympani
cold water drops on
splat-tapping
with a continuous cold beat
I don't know whether to be hardened to it
or tugged up to you immediately

the need for mother more desperate than thirst
to be cut from yourself at last— small flesh blob
in a barren universe
Your cry reminds me that there is a mountain top in me
where frozen air runs wild hands of longing
over an insatiable agony
o mother, mother
maaaaaa shouts the baby boy
maaaa the deep tree intones aching to its roots
maaaaa cries out the twisted steel of wrecks in the snow
of streetcar rails and cold untouched balconies
His cry pulls the golden plug from my breast
and contentment leaks out in a wild black gust
so that I am a bronze shell again bereft of sunshine

When he cries there is only one thing for a shadow to do
to connect with that baby
to rush up to him, cooing, comforting
talking to yourself
and lift him, all needy into the cradle of my arms
holding him til he quiets down
til both of us quiet down
til his quietness is a quietness in me.

Giant of the Cookycrumbs

When Charles Atlas lifted the mountains
my baby lifted up his eyes
and saw me
the horizon going over his head
like a forgotten umbrella
whole regions of sky hurled away from me
like a finally flung hat

As Charles held up the earth
my baby reached up his arms
to me
to stand
and I walked him
tall over towers
giant of the cookycrumbs
(through all the countries)
of the house

On hearing that Gandhi tested his Brahmacharya*
by sleeping with young girls**

What was it like lying with Gandhi
while he tested himself
What was it like to lie down
at night with perhaps the
GREATEST MAN WHO EVER LIVED
and not get a little tingle—
a silver little jet of LUST
somewhere, somewhere
in the testy northern Indian nights

God I love Gandhi
but I don't know whether I'd have wanted
him sleeping with my true love
though if she'd wanted to try "testing"
his Brahmacharya badly enough
I suppose I'd have no choice
"Come on" she'd say— "this is
possibly THE GREATEST MAN WHO EVER LIVED!"
and that would be it
I'd have nothing left to do but wish him luck
knowing already that he's a better man than I
who has never lasted the night
with her
yet.

*a Hindu vow of celibacy
**as reported by William L. Shirer, in the book *Gandhi: a memoir*

Love as though

Your mouth is the first mouth— the mouth I approach from the mountains, from the stars— swooping like a hawk to catch it turning, to catch it white and hot. Aaah breathe down deep into my substance and come away with a memory of the source of things— the river returning on itself with salmon and men. Come down by the falling water in me. Chip off all the old edges of your rigid life and come running again— in rocks and waves and winds til both of us are worn down— eroded to grains of sand— our bodies strewn over a thousand lands, lost in a million winds, on the boots even of the star travellers. Let us unravel mysteries long knotted and entwined on Fate's billion-fingered hand— gnarled about us like these winter trees. Let us come at last still patient to the poem in her palm— that simple verse— "Live and be happy"— from one another grow as though from a mutual soil— a replenishing rain-washed soil. Fertile in our touching and in our lovemaking. As though stones could not keep their shape and the moon depended on it. As though it had all come down to our love because it might all come down to our love.

Sleep Poem

I could be beside a thousand women
but I am beside you
I come down and lie beside the river
This is how stone sleeps, this is
how elephants sleep
   They come down all insomniac
and they listen to you
    soft river flowing
    they lie beside you and listen
and their breath calms down
And their heat calms down
lulled away by the rhythms
                    the currents
the mild winds, breathing
softer and softer
   bullrushes in your voice
breathing softer and softer
I could be lying beside
a cold mountain
I could lie by foreign forests
green with evening
I could lie by African lakes
deep in the motherland
close, close to the original
sleep
but I lie here—
   calmed by the sound
      of the stars
the deepness of the rivers
      in your dream
The countries are so vast there
and the love so true

I want to walk there
with you immediately, I don't
need a talisman— it is your hand
I touch in my fear
I lie down beside you
night after night
like the pages of the calendar
   steeped in dusk
thick sleep syrup in all the veins
the eyes wide open
I lie down by you
as though beside a terrible black cliff
with black wings by
an endless starless sky
I lie down by you like a road
and float away
The cars carry me away, the sound of horns
fades away
the whir of wheels takes me away
like the sound of sails
Your soft breathing blows me away
and when, like smoke the last tendrils
of mind are gone
the body, the dreamer
dreams

Difficult Heaven

Difficult heaven— a drop of rain— slides down the window held up only by friction, the buoyancy of earth-air. My true love has a difficult heaven in her thighs and I am the window holding her up for as long as I can. Soon she will be one with the dew, one with the water running rivulets down the houses and streets to the streams. Soon she will be one with the ocean crashing down and flattening out to a long streaming run up a beach. She and I keep afloat a difficult heaven by much heavy breathing, by many big words and miraculous acts. I can hold up an ocean on the tip of my tongue. I can pierce through a globe of dew and see a whole world come apart with a groan, everything sliding in its flat wash, wild up a smooth beach, huge vessels of delight. We are careening jugs, great urns of oil being spilled. We are jewels and barley scattered in the tide where gulls pick at us in a frenzy, gone and gone with our legs kicking up. You see how the rippling separates the sunset into a thousand flames? Well we are like that— life flows in and casts our Light into days and days, and our arms upraised, our bodies as we touch are just tributaries to it, reflections that must dance on the tide a while before they're drawn back into the lap of time.

poem cross canada

god glad to come safe back to you. Touch you my touchstone of flesh, each rivulet each line in the brown, each caress, each opening an entrance to love, a key, a combination in our touching opening something else something else. There is a wet flag flapping now in the country's long stomach, where wild hands go. I am exploring the myth in your belly, the dream that there is a wild black butterfly in there, wicked to get out, its wings flames, leaves of light that cannot flutter in the hurricane yet. God glad to come back safe to you. Nowhere has the land been so far away from its man, the land off in a boat— a bed in the darkness. The country awaiting its lad, its serf, its singer, spring waiting, summer waiting, everything ready for the man— the touch of a plane down in fog, the man landing, the whole earth waiting.

The Opening

The opening appeared one day in my mouth, because things sometimes just happen— clue things. So there's a moment when I realize that the ball of feeling that kept bobbing up in my chest is just lying there its long neck up my throat its mouth out my mouth— an opening into something— a thames swan, a dense womb-swan of some old suffering, a foetus in the throat soft as a heart, hard as a heart, waiting to be born, waiting to be born, and awful o that pulse in the bottom soft of the throat of the swan's throat. Cry out you honking bird, bird who swallowed my early life one thames day morning in old England where I walked on the riverside with my folks. Two giants, a dog and lo— a boy in shorts. Father throws stick— there are swans on the river, memory swans, eternal swans who suffer no capitulation to the customary amnesias. These ephemeral swans are floating by and the river is a kind of glorious suffering in the sun, a current of joy so deep in it, all agony is but reflection, but beautiful awful there in the English sun. So by some crystal motion in the day, in the magnitudes, the magnetics of it all, some soul-string-thing pulled them through and into me, this swan throat song that says uncover me, open up my eyes, and sing this thin song of the young, young days.

Babyness before Words

babyness before words, before there were cups, hats, hands to hold, just the liquid air, the heavy earth air that hung in everywhere, grievous in the lungs, making you cry. Call it loneliness, call it pranna. It hurt to breathe, or more to exhale for you always wish to keep it, then letting it go a cry is tugged out, a cry, and then *thwack!* the universal slap in the face that big brute, silence, no answer isolated, miles away on earth in a cradle in a room, in a room of rooms, down a hall in a heart in a dark in a terror I rocked, holding my hands and breathing it, and breathing it.

My Mother's Hands

They call me over the wilderness
over the waves, fingers in dials
fingers in rings, through keyboards of ivory
wringing themselves
bone dry
they call
that sewed with thimbles
those raw things, those dangerous hands
poet's, painter's hands, trapped in a woman
hands of mind, dripping with talent always talking
of slitting themselves open at the wrist
and just running away from it all
saying "sometimes I just feel like dying—"

In certain shapes memories are kept
flashing for a moment over the ages
as though from a genetic shore—
warnings, beauties, secrets
mother, mother—
this poem should be about your blood
your blood in the bath
threatening to be there
diluting the water behind the locked door
where you washed yourself making no sounds
"Mom"
as we lay awake in the room beside you
in our beds, calling out at regular intervals
"MOM"
just to make sure that life hadn't just slid out of you in there in a
slow freezing rush

Mother
this poem should be about the white of statues
the way you would say "this time I'm not coming back"
and walk away after arguments or blows,
 wrath, down the street
a long way to where it bends
and then turn
me praying, giving up preposterous rights
anything to god to jesus
to whatever it was that had the power to reassure me

Eventually she always came back
her hands freezing in the coat
having walked it off I suppose
cooled out
back
with a kiss
to show us
that brutality
can have the softest face
the most gentle hands
of all.

Zend Elegy

(on the publication of Robert Zend's posthumous *Daymares*)

Sadly like a flock of rectangular geese
papers migrate
cutting the air with a red grief
that Zend is gone so young
They were due for his many more poems
he was to give them a face, a shape
a place in time
but alas his hand has fallen silent like a rose
too much before its time and these are stories
that will never be
brilliance that won't shine
launched perhaps into the heavens
where beyond paper or substance
only angels will find them
clinging in rows of stars to the bottom of the rain
or the top of a cloud
anything to get down again
to time and a body

my friend Zend with the head full of popping seeds
walking around with his heart going bad on him
just laughing and reading his poems right to the end

in the height of his powers
the heart was weakest
in the full spring of his mind
he entered winter
darkness came and took
Zend away by the leg
his poor heart a dead weight it couldn't carry
so it took just the spirit
laughing and chanting high over the sad rooftop of his house

leaving only the gravity of his works and love
to draw us here together
over the page

In Memoriam: Ellen Priest

goodbye Ellen
how can you be dead
and England still there with all
its highlands and lakes
your wise eyes that lit up my early days
gone now— that much more smoke in the London air
London standing aggrieved
all its bridges black with your smoke
that rises at last free upon the breezes of this city
where you coughed your lungs out for years
the Thames like those long veins
in your legs

sweet Ellen the news saddens
three generations this side
of the ocean

so grandmother
with your gypsy blood
join your father and the generations
that cupped you or let you go
in the history now forgotten
now going on without you
with the leaves and autumn
and autumns to come all going
on without you
goodbye Ellen
who gave me my first knife
to eat with
a little knife
not sharp
but good to eat with
and had TV and chickens in the yard

so many times on your one visit
I framed you in memory
for goodbyes—
a side view of you in the back seat of the car
your profile aginst the moving window
that I will see forever
or touch like a piece of severed earth
from a land I love
mandala-like in the mind

even in your last days
you breathed the patriarch's black smoke
unable to use the common room at TV time
because some old codger was allowed to puff away there
coughing your guts out in that home
somewhere i'll not see now
living on so long
but gone now
2 months before my next visit

Everybody Gets Up...

Everybody gets up sometimes feeling like they have been burned in an atomic war. Waking up and there are a multitude of punctures in your heart and lungs through which unstoppable gusts of freezing air are being pumped. We all feel like useless cannon, abandoned instruments of rage or fury which we ourselves have cast down young, promising. Too many of us know that feeling of the heart tugged, nailed on to specific fences, pressed down under boulders over specific graves, my heart has been in the heart of the mountain, diamonds in its mouth that crushed with the fury, with the love and wonder of pressure, man, woman, what a sparkle in my eyes, to be fragmented like this, coming undone crystal by crystal til I am sand inside again, the vacant drifting in the eyes, the winds gathering and carving, knitting the needle eye in hunger and in weakness. The compression of this denial, dark in the spirit's dark ranges, this wealth at the bottom of the soul— this diamond of poverty and poetry.

The House behind the Theatre

In the house behind the theatre a very dramatic woman lived. She was always casting elaborate shadows on the walls, bringing up several children for just this purpose— sitting them just so with the husband. At night she would comb her long hair and watch how each strand of it was a strand of darkness on the wall and so part of the night— part of all night— combing the darkness out of her hair til she was light and her children too might be light. And so that wall became a kind of drama, a motion picture to her children where the play that determined their lives was acted out. Later, when they grew up, each of her children rejected her. One went off and lived with many other women, always cursing them, always waving good-bye while another adored women and crawled to get them. The third child, the youngest, was a woman herself and wandered in and out of that solitude, always a little horrified by her own body, shocked at her strange shape. Further and further they drifted each one in their own way forgetting almost all of their strange childhood in the process. Still whenever they walk in the night now, if they see the world cast on the sky, huge buildings against the moonlight and tall trees with gigantic shadows that seem to beckon and gesture, they pause and remember for a moment that woman with the dramatic hands.

Autumn of Hands

Autumn of hands, I fling these hands, over the rainbow, star-like, I fling these hands, these hands denied, these hands that grab the air, these hands that burn the bark off trees, I fling them from me, these sizzling octupi, these wrathful clutchers, unleashing their strangler's grip upon the lamp post, throat in the fence, a metal pole bending, I fling these hands that soar and explode, these hands of claw that gouge and shred your eyes, your belly, your bleeding guts, I hate these hands that gush darkness into the world, that bring the terror wriggling in these murderer's hands, these executioner's hands, these piano hands that bash your bones, these detonator digit snot-scraper crucifixion short-ribs, these blunt bleeding weapons, these iron dogs and elephant's tusks. These hands, denied. I hurl these hands I whip these hands I break them open and break them open and scrape these bones and sluice their giant's blood, these hated hands that are pinned up on city gates or hung from their veins in gallows. Sever these hands and hurl them from me and some of them whistle and some of them whirl. Some of them screech like jet planes and too many of them run off like warriors into the night, waiting out there for me or anyone with many many wrists like me. These hands that won't be gone, that come back like refugees, to wait sad and shuffling outside my door, thin, in rows like sheaves, one amongst the other in polarities, magnetic waves of fingers, seething, stitching, undulating.

Flag

The mind is a settled tapestry where thread has come unhooked and as I dart across in fear, as I go to get the milk I unknowingly unhook some of its delicate memories, its dream filaments and unravel them awhile as I wander, knitting random other scenes. See this black thread of my father, the dark vein of his name that unravels right through my own heart undoing something I thought strong in me with a single shiver? This is the dark thread of his touch which soon reaches its limit and yanks at its spindle— my heart, my heart. And here— this red thread of my mother, this green and dark thread that I spin round me as I dance. O this bleak white, same thread of a still blue painful day so long ago. There are just masses of it, huge piles of it loose as hair inside me. Sometimes you want to say— "Aaaah when it's all undone, do not weave me again onto a pattern of life. Do not knit again this Joseph robe of flesh, of nationalities and bloods onto my system." But you know if it was ever really ending you would do anything to have desire use its terrible needle again. "Aaaah I want to be shot through with life. There mustn't be a word left on the end of a string. All must interweave, leaping out of dark nights with white lips, tongues among the tongues. I must mix my lips with another's. Let our juices mix and create a new life. My hands are in your hands, desire. I have unravelled this much of my heart for you. Now will you take this red, this purple, this black, this green thread and run with me, one more time into the wind?"

A Cultural Nightmare

I had a nightmare and the secret police
came round and started to take away
the rock stars and pop song writers
rooster heads and shlock singers were detained
country gushers and the mock rock rebels
They came and they took them all away
Not for what they said
but for what they
didn't say.

Then they went and knocked on the doors
of prominent A&R men from the big record companies
and they dragged them screaming into waiting trucks
and drove away with them
Not because of the bands they had signed
but because there were certain bands
they wouldn't sing.

I watched with embarrassment as the poets quickly began
to write protest songs
but it was too late
They had to mean it.
It wasn't enough to do what others thought you should do
for that you could be shot, so
they were gathering them up north of Bloor
rooting them out of fairly large houses
and there was never such a wave of sick terror in the populace
Many finally called out things
screamed terrible truths into the night.
Those who had been constipated
shit all down their legs
and said "This can't happen in Rosedale!"
but it could and they were all taken away
not because of anything they did
but because of all the things they didn't do
the things they didn't say.

The Tree

(for Milton Acorn)

Once in the deep oak and maple magic of the forest an amazing seed was planted so that instead of a great oak, a man grew. Wild and full of poetry, full of the tug of the soil and the berry sun of summer this man absorbed a strange and powerful music from the bedrock beneath him, from the song of the water in the earth and the quick darting about of animals before him. And when the wind blew this man would wave his arms about positioning himself so that melody blew through his branches and leaves deep utterances, round wooden words, wide-mouthed rings of need, great oaken aches of loneliness so that the whole forest was moved by his song. "Sing, sing" they cried and he twisted and turned. He undulated his great branches through the sunlight causing strange shadow-plays in sunny groves. And then without warning a mighty bolt of lightning came crashing down out of the sky, splitting the stones about the tree, shattering the air about the tree, and wounding it from toe-tip to crown in a long fault-line of fire. Branches clutched branches but when the stone spoke in its great cracking voice, there was no protection from the sound. Screaming with pain the tree tugged its mighty roots like a tooth from the earth and ran off through the forest, maddening the wood with melody gone wrong, streaking the skies and the streams with blue need and anguish til it broke out in
a
clearing nearly
quiet and
close
to the
homes
of
men

The Environmental Leap Forward

I wake up and something amazing has happened to the parks. Something extraordinary has happened to those small squares and rectangles of trees and grass that has made them pop their borders, and spill out wildly exploding with green leaves, spear tips of grass and all sorts of uncontainable flowers, wild faunae, algae, and medicinal strange herbs. After the first immediate alarm in the populace, this miraculous event is rather too quickly assimilated into "public" consciousness by the glib news media. Compacted into a catch-phrase and left there, immaculate and explainable— it was a strange "twinge" in the environment. "An environmental leap." Nothing to worry about. Just as we evolve other things evolve "suddenly" and this was nothing but one of those periods for trees, grass, dandelions— dandelions everywhere impossible to weed out, great tangles of yellow sun-seeking dandelion heads butting at bank buildings and knocking over stop signs. The question now is how to get it all back to normal. How to begin clearing away these immense forests which have covered the canyons and prairies of everywhere everywhere and reassert the primacy of roads, ploughed fields, subdivisions, industry.

II.

We have amazing images of the twinge that rocked nature. We have on video the burst of buds, the javelin hurl of poplars up to the point of that one highest blade of green quivering in the blue wind. Yes yes, and look at the blur of these lianas, gentians and violets. They are like purple blasts of rocketry each blossom a trail of power left by something that has departed. Wow. And here is the mango grove that toppled the space fields of Florida, tangling up astronauts and gardeners alike in sweet exacerbating blossoms. I suppose everyone everywhere will always remember just where they were the day the greenery went wild. The night when nature throbbed. Life throbbed.

III.

Despite several years of effort in the tangled amazons of the River Don the Toronto government has been unsuccessful in re-establishing the former Riverdale Park. Despite a massive government work plan to log the fabulous area and plant sod, efforts have been foiled again and again by the re-growth and the undergrowth of the powerful new foliage. Recently a bold new plan has been put forth by City Council to "integrate the city into the already existing environment."

Modified Famous Phrases*

(or: Butcher Slogans not People!)

We can put a man on the moon but we can't
STOP THE WAR

If wishes were horses beggars would
STOP THE WAR

Don't pick your nose or your eyes will
STOP THE WAR

Spare the rod and
STOP THE WAR

It takes a lot to laugh but it takes a train to
STOP THE WAR

Forgive and
STOP THE WAR

To gain the world and
STOP THE WAR

I liked this new stainless steel razor blade so much I had to go out
and
STOP THE WAR

*This poem is intended for use at demonstrations. The leader would call out the beginning of the famous phrase and the others would respond with the modified ending. Other famous phrases could be added, of course, and there might be many more modified endings, such as "Stop ailments!" or "Ban pesticides."

Fictinos: Time Release Poems

(or: More slogans, sayings, corrections, koans and connections)

Whitewash comes in many colours
*

Busy in the many with many hats
and nothing to put them on
*

No matter which way you turn
there's always something you're not facing
*

There is no peace for the punching bag
*

True marksmen see beyond guns
*

Too much time is wasted in the making of clocks
*

Every little ruler wants a 13th inch
*

There is no camouflage like a good philosophy
*

One wind moves many flags
*

Daylight respects no borders
*

Cars— people fleeing in their problems
*

Clothes make the man— poor
*

The teacher *is* the lesson
*

If you would see a parent
look in the eyes of the child
*

That is like setting yourself on fire
in order to see in the dark
*

To burn a good cook
*

To read by the light of burning pianos

*

To hide a pin prick in a sword's thrust
*

To dirty your hands washing your gloves
*

To laugh at your own teeth
*

To cry for the thirsty
*

To cut bread with a dagger
*

To fear the gun and butter too
*

To break one egg with another
*

To carry an egg in too many baskets
*

All package no content
*

All edge no interior
*

All interior no edge (infinity)
*

The last number is affinity
(Eli Kirzner-Priest— age 4)
*

Forgive and remember
*

Never say "Never say never."
*

When you deny you deny you deny!
*

Ignorance is blight
*

A little bit of knowledge is a beginning
*

You can't go down from the bottom
*

There is no trampoline like the bottom of the soul

*

The edge comes from within
*

Home is where the heat is
*

Do you travel for the journey
or just for the arrival?
*

Different destinations
but for a while the same path
*

If the poison don't get you the antidote will
*

If the famine don't get you the feast will
*

If the celibacy don't get you—
*

Good lovers come in pairs
*

There is no balance without opposition
*

You cannot kiss ass and kick it too
*

You can't make tea without water
(Marsha Kirzner)
*

You can't murder the dead
*

You can't forgive yourself
without forgiving others
*

A sweet tongue won't cure a rotten tooth
*

There is nothing worse for men than overcoming giants
*

The most dangerous people are the obedient
*

Quislings with no Reich

*
To blow out the match and the candle too
*
When the last light goes out
what is the speed of darkness?
*
Don't call your own shadow the night
*
Don't love the rose only for its thorns
*
Don't sharpen the arrow as it hits you
*
Sooner your hat than your head.
*
A day is only as bright as the people in it
*
Resolution not revolution
*
The peace you make may be your own
*
Not just PEACE but a JUST peace
*
The only peace is JUSTICE
*
Justice not justification
*
We're bigger than all of us
*
I can see the planet in your eyes
*
The only promise is doing
*
Sometimes being mixed up
makes the cake
*

Homebirth

coming down to a holy land
coming through the holiest domain
in a bedroom on bain ave.
elegantly believe me—
the room seems to pulse with shadow-circles
contraction rings about the moon
shuffling and shuffling
quietly with the right cries
the right sounds of anguish
pushing out this urgent passenger
freely into the world
two mid-wives and Jaylene
make a ring of magic
with their hands—
til
a milk-white bubble emerges— some fabulous jewel!
an amazing moonstone she has carried all milky
over fabulous borders to bring out here, aching and triumphant
What is this glowing crystal
She pushes.
"It is good that your system makes such
strong membranes."
Eli, the four-year-old, saying—
"Push! You pushed me out
so you can push this one out too."
Casual as though she were unearthing melons.
a woman of crystal bringing forth a crystalline orb
a child within
then the bubble bursts shooting forth its amniotic milk
with an awful tear of anguish in her voice
she pushes again
and the brown flesh of the skull appears
amazing—
the shadows shimmer in circles round the room

the world is contracting
we are peering in in wonder
til another mighty shove brings the newborn head halfway,
already breathing, through the widened ring of her vagina
unswallowing this tiny human
the head is out, another push— a miracle all of us gasping
this whole new being still attached to the inside
by a long white cord is out
slippery hot in my hands
all curled in instinct
a tense question mark
i carry terrified ecstatic
to her breasts
and wait

Index of Previous Publication

FROM *THE VISIBLE MAN*
(Unfinished Monument, 1979)

Revolutions 11
Friend 12
Poem for Ursula in New York 13
Poem 14
Translations 15
Meditation on a Ruler 16
Cigarettes 17
The Door Knob 18
The Hammer 18
Flags 19
What Dew Is 20
Little Heart of My Heart 21
The Change 22
You Want Her 23
If 24
Signatures 25
A Tall Man Walking Fast 25
What Ugly Is 26
On Genuflection 27
Mommies 28
Are There Children 30
An Unidentified Man 31
Target Practice 32
Lesser Shadows 33
The Re-assembled Atom 35
Excuses 36
Concerning My Obsession
     with Blood 37
A Poem about Water 38
Ode to the Clitoris 39
Ode to the Penis 40
Ode to the Bum 41
To His 20th Century Lover 41
Poem for a Dark Woman 42
When My Faith Leaps 43
Birth 44
Slight Exaggeration of a Childhood
     Incident 45
Adolescence 46
My Grandfather Lives 48
My Infected Rainbow 49
Crumbs 73
Disguises 78
The Longer Bed 80

FROM *SADNESS OF SPACEMEN*
(Dreadnaught, 1980)

Candles 50
The Man behind the Bees 51
The Retroactive Orphan 53
The Ancestry 54
Thirst 55
The Childhood Pin 56
His Little Mother 57
My Therapeutic Cock 58
On the Assembly Line 59
Astrology and the Blood Shadow 60
All the Sounds a Scared
     Man Hears 61
Why You Have the Maps 62
Sadness of Spacemen 63
The Television 64
Sultan of the Snowflakes 65
Points 66
The Cup of Words 67
The Kiss I Just Missed 68
Since You Left 69
Hold Me 70
Come to Me 72
Ode to Your Mouth 74
Falling through the Heart 75
Insomnia 79
My Father's Hands 134

FROM *THE MAN WHO BROKE OUT*
OF THE LETTER X
(Coach House, 1984)

Cherries 81
Peaches 82
Mangoes 83
Dec. 8, 1980 84
Ghost Removal 86
How to Pray to a Woman 87
How to Pray to a Toilet 88
Christ Is the Kind of Guy 90
Getting Close to God 92
The Starved Man 93
Questions about the Wine 94
Oppress the Oppressed 95
Testament of a New Faith 96

Go, Gather Up the Love   97
Blue Pyramids   98
In the Next War   99
Report on the Earth-Air Addicts   101
The Arms Race of Obbagga   102
Paper   104
Paper II   105
Secrets of Paper   106
Ink   107
Literary Party   108
The Escaped Cock   109
The Uncatchable Man   111
Moth   113
My Body   114
Tales of a Domestic Heart   116
Poem for a Tall Woman   118
Now There Is Rain   119
The Man with the Nitroglycerine
Tears   120
Sometimes There Is a Way   121
Eggshell Children   122
The School behind the School   123
Poète   124
Adventures of My Hand   125
The Man Who Broke Out
of the Letter X   126

FROM THE MAD HAND
(Coach House, 1988)

Proposal   76
More!   77
Sweet and Sour Angel Wings   89
Beautiful Money   100
The Grizzums   103
Precautionary Chandeliers   110
Poem for a Fisherwoman 1983   115
The Birth of a Tree   127
The Mad Hand   128
My Huge Voice   130
Fear of Hands I   131
Fear of Hands II   133
In Stupid School   135
I Knew I Could Sing (Industrial
Accident No. 1)   136
Why I Crushed My Hand   137
Industrial Accident No. 2   139
Little Hurts   140
The Violent Man's Hand   141

Poetry Is...   142
Colours of Bullshit   143
Several Other Uses for a Halo   144
In Drug Heaven   146
To Me, Eating a Piece of Meat   147
My Problem with the Flag   148
My Problem with the Canadian
National Anthem   149
Silence Is Coming   150
Consumption   151
My Infected Television   153
The Little Pig of Self Respect   154
An Exhortation to Dance   155
sperm sperm sperm   157
The Origin of "Woman"   158
Poem for My Unborn Child   159
On the Birth of My Son   160
New Father   160
Your Cry   161
Giant of the Cookycrumbs   163
On hearing that Gandhi tested his
Brahmacharya by sleeping with
young girls   164
Love as though   165
Sleep Poem   166
Difficult Heaven   168

NEW POEMS

poem cross canada   169
The Opening   170
Babyness before Words   171
My Mother's Hands   172
Zend Elegy   174
In Memoriam: Ellen Priest   175
Everybody Gets Up...   177
The House behind the Theatre   178
Autumn of Hands   179
Flag   180
A Cultural Nightmare   181
The Tree   182
The Environmental
Leap Forward   183
Modified Famous Phrases   184
Fictinos: Time Release Poems
(also from
The Man Who Broke Out of the Letter X
and The Mad Hand)   185
Homebirth   189